Sue

Sue

Kurth Krause

2024

Copywrite 2024 by Kurth Krause

All rights reserved. No part of this publication may be reproduced, distributed, or transmitted in any form or by any means, or stored in a database, or retrieval system without the prior written consent of the publisher and author.

Cover design by Taylor Odish

ISBN 978-0-4568-81

Contents

1. The Soul Mate 1
2. The Occupational Therapist 39
3. The Mother 43
4. The Artist 59
5. The Philanthropist 77
6. The Golfer 83
7. The Cowgirl 89
8. The Christian 97
9. The Home Decorator 101
10. The World Traveler 107
11. The Granny 179
12. The Surgery Patient 191

Epilogue 197

Preface

On November 20, 2023, I lost my wife, my lover, and my best friend after 60 years of marriage. I was bewildered. I was not prepared. I thought I would die first, even though Sue was not as heathy as I. Sue was a stronger Christian than I was. Why would God take her first? Maybe He delayed my passing so that I could author this book to preserve her memory forever.

The 25 days I spent with Sue in the hospital deepened our incredible relationship even more than I thought possible. It better prepared me not only for her passing, but also my own mortality. I will be prepared to join Sue in heaven for eternity when the time comes. Until then, I will embrace the memories of our time together recorded in this book.

Originally, I intended to write the memoir of Sue's remarkable life chronologically, but instead chose topically. So many of Sue's interests and accomplishments spanned so many years that I decided to concentrate these attributes in chapter topics to emphasize each. I hope this viewpoint gives you, the reader, a true perspective of this incredible human being.

1. The Soul Mate

I met the love of my life, Susan Ruth Firle, my sophomore year on the student train going to the 1960 University of Wisconsin Rose Bowl. It took 48 hours to get from our boarding station in Chicago to Los Angeles. I was traveling with eleven of my Alpha Delpha Phi fraternity brothers, never anticipating that this would be the most important milestone of my life. The train consisted of several cars of female students and a like number of male student cars separated by a bar car full of Schlitz beer. This, being 1959 when sexual morality was required by the conservative Midwest parents, the female cars were segregated from the males to ensure we would not be sleeping together. Schlitz had donated the beer for the students, but we were required to pay a 25 cent surcharge per can for the gratuity. I'm sure this was encouraged by the university as a deterrent to rowdy behavior onboard. We were warned that the bar car would be closed when we traversed New Mexico which was dry due to the Sunday Blue Laws. But that was not a deterrent as we simply stocked up before we left Texas.

But we did commingle during the daylight hours. That's when I met Sue. She joined other girls in visiting our car. I was immediately attracted to this pretty, petite blonde with a nice figure and beautiful brown eyes. But the thing that I noticed first was her radiant smile. It seemed to light up the train car. I soon learned that smile was her trademark.

Sue at Nineteen

We quickly hit it off. This attraction was enhanced when I learned she belonged to a country club and drove an MG (her mother's car). I learned she was a good golfer with a respectable handicap, while I was just a publinx beginner.

Somehow, we were not tired when we reached Los Angles despite the grueling 48 hour train ride. We twelve Alpha Delts rented two cars and began our California adventure. Most of us had not been outside the Midwest, so we took advantage of the next two days to see as much of LA as possible. Our first stop was Venice to see the Beatniks we'd heard so much about, and to see the amazing Pacific Ocean. Next was the Sunset Strip and the famed Copacabana restaurant, The following day, after checking out the famous Brown Derby, we actually hopped the fence at Universal Studios and got away with it by one of our guys making believe he was a tour guide, pointing out items of interest on the sets.

We concluded the second day by going to a party hosted by a female student who lived in Beverly Hills adjacent to Debby Reynolds' home and on the same street as Elizabeth Taylor's. I was overjoyed to spend more time with my new girlfriend whom I again met at the party. I spotted her trademark smile immediately as she seemed to light up the enormous living room. We were all amused by the butler in full dress tuxedo tidying up the home by picking up the empty beer cans. Rock and roll music permeated the mansion. But the party ended abruptly when someone set off an alarm. The knock on the door by the police told our hostess that the house was surrounded, suggesting an end to our frivolities.

I spent the third day with Sue at Disneyland. The admission tickets were part of the Rose Bowl package. In those days, the rides were designated "A" through "E," according to the excitement and quality of the ride. We each had coupons contained in the admission book with an allocation for each type of ride. My favorite ride was the Mad Hatter Teacups. Each person sat in a circle around a center steering wheel, which enabled anyone onboard to spin the cup as fast as they liked. I tried to get Sue dizzy, but she loved it.

That night I walked over to pick Sue up at her hotel. The girls were in the Alexandria Hotel, the guys across Pershing square in the Biltmore. Once again, we were segregated at night to preserve our chastity. We attended an all-night movie that added some extra entertainment. Some guy a few rows down was sound asleep, snoring so loudly that we almost couldn't hear the dialog. Finally, a woman behind us marched down the aisle alongside of him, clapped her hands together, and woke him up, ending his concert. Later we heard a load clattering as something rolled down the steps from the projection booth. One of the projectionists had dropped a can housing the movie reel.

The next night was New Year's Eve. Sue and I danced the night away. She let me sing in her ear and pretended to enjoy it. After midnight we retreated to a large open room in the hotel with several other couples sprawled across the floor until the chaperones broke it up.

The next morning, we were all up at 6:30 for the bus trip to the Rose Parade in Pasadena. Once again, I found Sue, bundled up to brave the cold morning weather, as we viewed the spectacular parade side by side. Then we walked to the Rose Bowl stadium for the game. We were surprised that we students had such great seats near the 50 yard line. Ronald Reagan and his wife were seven rows above us; Richard Nixon and his wife were six rows in front of us. We lost the game, but that was anticlimactic. I had just spent the time of my life with a girl with which I was falling in love.

The forty-eight hours on the train home was more fun since they let our girls occupy our car overnight. I think the smile on my face became permanent.

I did have a problem when we returned to Madison. I was dating another girl on campus who lived in Sue's dormitory. They knew each other and, to my detriment, enjoyed comparing notes on their dates with me. I also was dating two other girls in my hometown of Milwaukee. Sue solved my problem many months later. After a fraternity drinking game in which we each chugged three cans of beer, she gave me an ultimatum: drop the other three girls and date only Sue or she was dumping me. I really liked the other girls, but she made the decision easy -- best decision ever.

Eventually we played golf together – a humiliating experience. She really did know how to play golf. It was clear that I did not. I learned that she began to play at age eight with professional tutelage. I made up my mind to learn to play at her level, but that would not happen for another eight years. Very humbling.

I discovered that, although Sue was not a big drinker, she had a reputation for holding her own. She liked to show off her beer-drinking prowess at the "Var Bar" (Varsity Bar) just off campus. This tiny girl could actually win a chug-a-lug contest by downing a full pitcher of beer faster than anyone. She could open her gullet and pour it right down!

Sue was unable to pledge a sorority her freshman year because she came down with mononucleosis during rush season. But when I was elected president of the Alpha Delta Phi Wisconsin Chapter in 1961, she became our first lady, easily adopted by all my fraternity brothers. I was overjoyed to parade her around the Greek community. She no longer had a need or interest in joining a sorority. She loved all our fraternity parties, as did I. At the end of our junior school year, she accepted wearing my fraternity pin, signifying us as an exclusive couple. I couldn't be happier.

Alpha Delta Phi was the only fraternity with a boat house on Lake Mendota. The alumni had the old house torn down and a new one built in its place with a dance floor on top of the boat house. Therefore, our house was great for the many dances we held there. Sue loved to dance, especially East Coast Swing. One Saturday night we featured the popular Kingston Trio.

Formal Alpha Delta Phi Party with Elegant Sue in First Row

She also wild about our elaborate theme parties. For the Rites of Spring, we delivered invitations, written on bones, to their dorms. We filled the fraternity party room with sand and fresh-cut cedar fencing. We all dressed in animal skins and boarded a raft to traverse Lake Mendota to the party site. There we conducted exciting games including daring the girls to catch a greased pig. Sue enjoyed playing with my bongos, but she rejected the greased pig. Then we actually roasted another large pig which tasted terrific, washed down with the kegs of beer. We reboarded the rafts to return to

Smelly animal skins, no smiles

the fraternity house for fun and games on the sandy party floor.

We also dressed up for a western hoedown.

Sue always looked great in costume.

We had a resident housemother, Mrs. Sullivan, an elderly widow who kept us in line. She loved Sue and they became good friends.

Sue attended summer school after her junior year to earn six more credits. She elected to stay at the Alpha Delta Phi fraternity house which we leased out to pay for our mortgage during the down months. She proudly announced that she would stay in my room during the summer.

Sue's grade-point average increased during our junior year while mine suffered. We spent many study dates in the library's stacks. It was apparently a good influence on her study habits; mine – not so much. But my grades were still high enough to be accepted to graduate school in physics. We both graduated with honors in June 1962.

I asked Sue to marry me upon graduation. She accepted as I gave her the best engagement ring I could afford. She acted like she loved it. But she proceeded to temporarily

Sue's Graduation Picture

lose it immediately after she received it. Ouch!

I warned that we would never be wealthy. But as an engineer, we would be comfortable, living on my salary as an employee.

While Sue satisfied her residency requirements for her occupational therapy certification, I began my year of graduate school. We continued to date whenever her schedule allowed. But so many weeks apart were not easy for either of us.

Towards the end of the academic year, I began interviewing with several companies around the country who recruited on the Wisconsin campus. I knew I would receive an offer from the aerospace division of General Motors in Milwaukee. I had previously worked there in the summers. But I wanted to see what else was out there. I had never been on an airplane, so I enjoyed flying to both the East and West Coasts for interviews. My best offer was from a growing company in Redondo Beach California. When I suggested to Sue that we forego our plans to settle in Milwaukee and accept this attractive offer, I learned about her adventurous spirit. She jumped at the idea and was ready to go to California, leaving our Wisconsin roots behind. Thinking it over, I suggested following through with our plans to live in Milwaukee after we were married and deferring the California alternative for now. Sue seemed a bit disappointed, but we would have many opportunities to satisfy her taste for adventure.

She soon experienced a different adventure. I received a call from her as I was buried in final exams, telling me the there was a problem with my car, a 1957 Volkswagen Beetle. I had lent it to her to travel home to Fond du Lac, Wisconsin. She had to be towed the final 20 miles. She informed me that the engine was now in a box in the front seat, and they didn't know what the problem was with the transmission. With the help of my dad, who negotiated a trade-in value of $400, I bought a new 1963 VW Beetle for $1900, almost wiping out the savings I had accumulated from my summer jobs.

Sue continued to blossom during our engagement.

Unfortunately, she introduced me to a terrible habit. We both smoked nearly one pack per day. We made a vow to quit when we married. But we both smoked our last cigarette on the way to the church.

We married on June 15, 1963, in her hometown of Fond du Lac. Sue was a radiant bride.

The Happiest Day of My Life

But it began with some trauma as Sue's brother-in-law threw me in the pool with my tuxedo on at the reception at her father's country club. She did not share my trauma. She could not stop laughing.

That afternoon we were sent off by the crowd for our honeymoon in our new Volkswagen with old shoes, ballons, and a sign attached to the car.

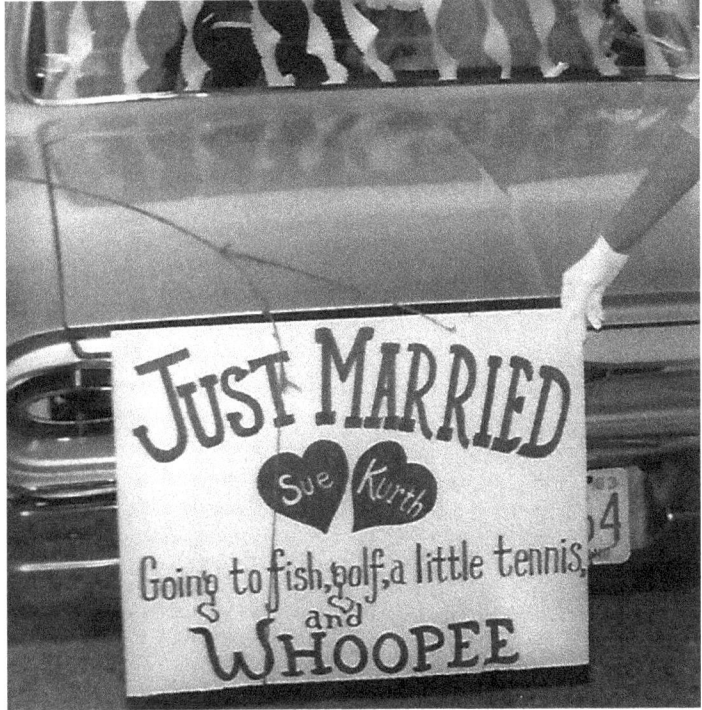

We actually drove to our honeymoon with this attached to our car.

We drove to Door County, Wisconsin's vacation and honeymoon peninsula for a great week. We did indeed play golf -- 90 holes at the three courses on the peninsula. We also went fishing and attended several nightclubs, where we were spotted as newlyweds.

I learned my new wife not only knew how to play golf, but also knew how to fish, and she didn't think baiting the hook was *gross*. Years later, I would learn just how good she was.

I started work and Sue returned to her job as an occupational therapist the following Monday. But a few weeks later I took up smoking again. Sue was strong and quit for good, while I struggled with the habit. She learned her OT duties were simpler when she did not have a cigarette to deal with. I only quit twelve years later. It was the hardest thing I ever overcame.

I quickly learned what a great pair we made. We were 100% compatible and grew more in love as the years went by. Yet we were Yin and Yang. Sue was right-brained; I was left. Sue was spontaneous, adventurous and fun. I was thoughtful, logical, and careful. She loved nature and art. I was enamored with the science and physics of the universe. So, we really complimented each other's strengths and weaknesses, resulting in true compromises that worked for both of us, enabling a wonderful life together. We did have common interests: family, golf, and travel. But I believe our real strength was our ability to listen to each other's ideas and different points of view. Our marriage was a 50/50 partnership. We learned so much from the other's dominant part of the brain that we never made a unilateral decision. But Sue was definitely the better half because of her penchant for the wellbeing of other people. She made friends so easily.

My upbringings caused me to be careful with money, saving whenever possible. Sue like to shop, saving money by spending (whenever she could find a sale). We respected each other's intellect. Once one of our friends asked Sue what it is like to be married to a genius. She immediately responded, "Why don't you ask him?"

The Apollo Era

In September 1967 we moved into our home in El Lago Texas, four miles from the Johnson Space Center. Soon after we moved in, we discovered our backyard was infested with snails. Instead of revulsion, Sue saw this as an opportunity. We had acquired a taste for escargot. She gathered up over two hundred of the critters and fed them cornmeal. But when it was time to prepare them as a delicacy, she realized she did not know how to cook them, In frustration, she released the little guys into the garbage can.

Sue decided our home would be a real party house. She loved hosting theme parties and usually went over the top with decorations.

We had fun living among the Apollo astronauts when we lived in El Lago. Sue made great life-long friends with some of the astronauts' wives. Charlie and Dotty Duke lived across our cul-de-sac. Bill and Val Anders were next to the Dukes. Our next-door neighbors were Ron and Jan Evans. Jerry and JoAnn Carr lived around the corner. Neil and Jan Armstrong lived on our street, Woodland Drive. All would become famous before we left El Lago eight years later.

When Bill Anders returned home from orbiting the moon on Apollo 8 on Christmas eve in 1968, Val Anders called Sue to invite us to Bill's homecoming party. When Bill met us at the door, I told him, "Bill, I heard you were out of town during the holidays." Sue was not the only one with quips. Bill sent us this First Day Cover announcing man's first visit to the moon.

Commemorating Man's First Orbit of the Moon in December 1968

Bill took this picture of the beautiful earth as he orbited the moon. It soon became famous.

One day in July 1969, Dotty Duke called Sue to tell her Charlie had secured passes for us at the astronaut viewing area for the Apollo 11 launch. My employer TRW was excited for us. They granted me the time off and arranged for pre-launch party invitations at the Cape. We were lucky to reserve the last two seats on National Airlines to Orlando. All the hotels had been booked for weeks. But friends Romily and Lois Gilbert offered to put us up at their home in Titusville. Rom was supporting the launch from the Kennedy Space Center control room but was unable to get parking passes for his family. So, we asked them to accompany us in our rental car. Our neighbors volunteered to take our toddlers, Scott and Sheryl, and we were off to the Cape for the most historic launch ever.

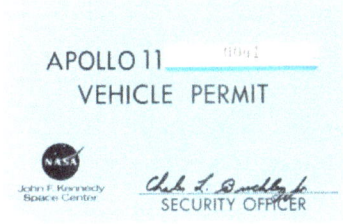

Pass Allowing VIP Parking

We used our passes to park our car on the NASA causeway, but Rom's family had to watch from the car. We walked ½ mile past the Vertical Assembly Building bleachers, where Lyndon Johnson, Johnny Carson, over 200 congressmen, and other VIP dignitaries were seated. The astronaut viewing area was not luxurious. We joined a small party of astronaut family and friends. We met Charles Lindberg and Alan Shepherd there. We were issued small American flags and bottles of water.

Our concern of a launch delay quickly dissipated as the clouds parted and the engines began firing. Since we were three miles away, we did not hear the thunderous sound of the launch until the mighty Saturn V had left the tower. Then the sound enveloped us and shook the ground. The launch was a spectacular success! Sue painted this picture when we returned to Houston.

Sue's Painting of the Launch of Apollo 11

NASA invited me to support the mission in the Mission Operations Control Room at the Johnson Space Center during the 13 minute powered descent to the moon. It was the most exciting time of my life!

Less than three years later, it was Charlie's turn to pilot the lunar landing spacecraft on Apollo 16. Once again Charlie secured a parking pass for us to view the launch. This time we drove to the Cape with the kids. We were not sure Sheryl was old enough to understand what was really going on until she waved as the stack left the launch pad and said, 'Goodbye Mr. Duke."

Charlie took mementos down to the lunar surface, brought them back, and presented them to us. He had the flag of Texas mounted with a collage of his picture on the moon and the Apollo 16 logo, and wrote, "To Sue and Kurth, two wonderful friends and neighbors. With sincere best wishes. [signed] Charlie Duke."

Charlie created this collage including the Texas flag from the moon.

He also presented Sue with a pendant of the Lunar Module brought back from the lunar surface. Inscribed on the back of the pendant is "To Sue from Charlie via Descartes."

Our next-door neighbor, Ron Evans, was the Command Module Pilot for the last moon flight, Apollo 17. Sue decided to have a send-off party at our home for Ron and his wife, Jan, the night before his departure to the Cape. The neighbors got the great idea to embellish this night. They planted a hidden one-way microphone (transmit, but not receive) in the Evans bedroom. Ron and Jan had farmed out their kids so they could have a romantic night alone. We all gave them appropriate gag gifts for their special night. They went home early. So, after 20 minutes, we began: "Oh, Ron. What a performance! Jan, you were great. So much energy!" Ron crawled into his attack to extract the offending microphone.

The next morning at 6:30 at the foot of our bed, we awoke to find ourselves looking up at the barrel of Ron's shotgun, while Jan videoed us with the NASA camera. That day we all went to Ellington AFB to see Ron off in his T-38. He began taxiing down the runway, then suddenly made a right turn pointing the T-38 needle nose directly at us! After we scattered, he continued his

Apollo 17 First Day cover Honoring all the Apollo Flights

takeoff. They succeeded in getting back at us. But he did send us this great memento of the history of Apollo. Sue loved it.

Jerry Carr invited us to the launch of the last Apollo Command Module to rendezvous with the Skylab Space Station, but we were unable to attend. Jerry was the commander of the last Skylab mission in 1973-4.

*****

In 1970, I discovered another of Sue's passions the first time we went to Las Vegas. We landed at 10 pm and immediately went to our hotel, the Tropicana. Sue sat down at the first slot machine at the entrance and began to play an all-jackpot nickel machine. I left her to check in, then sat down at the adjacent machine and began to play, noticing she was winning some nickels. After an hour, I told her I was going to bed; she said she would be right along. I awoke at 8 am, but Sue was not in the room. I showered, got dressed and went down to find Sue. She was at the same machine, now pulling the lever with her left hand because her right arm was sore. Her tray was filled with nickels, and her fore-arms were black! I finally convinced her to stop, cash out, and go to our room. When we finished breakfast, she returned to HER machine, and was incensed that someone had taken her spot.

As we matured as small-time gamblers, Sue played blackjack but preferred the slots in casinos on our cruises and in Southern California as well as Las Vegas. We frequently stayed at the Golden Nugget, the Tropicana, and the Wynn. Sue loved the spectacular shows at the Wynn. Her favorite dining experience was Hugo's Celler at the Four Queens. She always enjoyed the myriad of chosen ingredients for the salad which the waiter tossed flamboyantly as we watched. We usually shared a prime rib entre. But she loved the flambe desserts.

Soul Mate in California

We moved our family to Costa Mesa California September 1975. Even though it meant leaving our exciting days in Texas, Sue was ready for another new adventure. The children were not happy about leaving their school and friends in Texas, but they easily adapted. Sue brought her newly acquired etching talent and quickly became immersed in life in Southern California and broadened her interests in so many ways. It didn't seem possible that she could acquire so many skills and succeed at them, but she did.

We joined Mesa Verde Country Club, and it became a major source of our entertainment for the next 44 years. Charlie and Dotty Duke visited us there.

Sue and Dotty at Mesa Verde Country Club

Sue reveled in Mesa Verde's many parties. Some were theme parties that were always a big favorite for Sue. Each summer we attended a wine tasting event, featuring almost 100 wineries. It was called Concert on the Green. The seafood hors d oeuvres, steak entrees, and exquisite deserts never disappointed. The excellent band delighted everyone.

Each year, the club's highlight was always New Years Eve.

New Year's Eve at MVCC

Annual New Year Photo at Mesa Verde

Another highlight of our 44 years as members of MVCC occurred when Tiger Woods decided to host his annual invitational golf tournament at the club, a fund raiser for his TGR Foundation for inner city children. Mesa Verde was the first private club at which six-year-old Tiger played golf. Even though he chose to play from the back tees, he shot 98. The PGA seniors did not play from the back tees for their inaugural Toshiba tournament in 1995, because their scores would be too high. Five PGA tournaments and six LPGA tournaments had been held at MVCC. Tiger did not play in the fundraiser, but he and Freddie Couples did put on a clinic for the amateur tournament participants and the members. The Board of Directors were invited to a photo shoot with Tiger and Freddie prior to their warmup for the clinic. This was how I had my picture taken with Woods.

Kurth and Tiger at MVCC

Although Sue loved watching the clinic, the real thrill for her was taking part in Tiger's Block Party at the Anaheim Convention Center that night. All Board Members and their wives were invited. Sue was thoroughly entertained by the Eagles band, who she had never seen in person before. She also enjoyed bidding on the live auction for the first class tickets to the Masters tournament and the British Open. We dropped out of the bidding well before each reached $40,000. Woods raised over one million dollars for the event.

Each Board member was invited to present one item for Tiger's autograph. This was no small gesture because each autographed item in the silent auction at the Anaheim Convention Center started the bidding at $1,000. But Sue persuaded me to submit **two** items because we had two local grandchildren. She bought two TW golf caps. At first, only one was returned with his autograph, but six months later I received the second one. He added something: "Best Wishes, Tiger Woods."

Sue joined a wonderful local ladies club called Los Alegres in Costa Mesa. They organized a great party at least once each year.

Years later, Sue did accept my decision to retire when I was 58. Conditionally. She quipped "Okay, but I'm not making breakfast, and I'm not making lunch. But I will make reservations for dinner!" I loved it.

Life in Reata Glen

Sue wanted to join a retirement community that offered nursing services onsite. While I knew she was logically correct that this would be the right thing to do in our senior years, I thought we were too young and didn't need to commit to the expense until we were older. I am so happy that I listened to her. We moved to the Reata Glen Continuing Care Retirement Community as soon as it was built in 2019. It was exactly the right decision!

We met so many wonderful people soon after we moved in. Sue acquired dozens of close friends. Life here was much better than I expected. We moved in to a small three-bedroom villa on the campus, requiring us to downsize by almost 50%. We have a good view from our backyard patio:

Good View from Our Backyard Patio

The Reata Glen clubhouse is ¼ mile from our home. Between the gym, the many exercise classes, water aerobics, and the walk, I get the necessary daily exercise. I also attend the weekly line dance lessons, the ballroom dance classes, the Rooted classes, and the karaoke rehearsals.

The monthly live concerts, dances, poker games, and frequent popular movies in the theater provide many opportunities for entertainment. Most importantly the wonderful residents at Reata Glen are available for evening meals, cocktail parties, and just socializing on a daily basis.

Our first big party here was Halloween. All the residents and the staff dressed in costume. Sue bought masks so we could attend as Laurel and Hardy. No one recognized us, but we won first prize, a $50 gift certificate.

First Prize Winners

Sue and I played duplicate bridge here weekly. She earned her Bronze Life Master rating from the American Contract Bridge League in 2017. She and her Japanese partner won their division's duplicate bridge competition one year, resulting in a paid trip to the ACBL National Tournament representing the local club.

The Reata Glen community was voted the best in Orange County for each of the past three years. It also provides transportation to local churches, doctors, shopping, and excursions. If I ever lose my California driving privileges, this service will be invaluable.

We had two cars when we moved in but found it inconvenient to have one car in our small driveway with the other in the garage. At first, Sue was reluctant to part with her precious red Jaguar, but then learned to love to drive my Tesla. She particularly liked its amazing acceleration and large screen in the cockpit. Sue always had a soft spot for any sports car. Her first was a Plymouth Road Rummer in the 1970s. Then she bought a flashy two-tone Supra before buying her first and second Jaguars. Her adventurous demeanor surfaced again.

Every month Reata Glen offers excursions throughout Southern California. We attended several local plays and performances.

Sue and I were fervent football fans and followed the Green Bay Packers and Wisconsin Badgers religiously. Each time the Packers played, Sue hung their flag outside our front porch. But if they lost, I draped a shroud over it. We had attended two tours of Lambeau Field; so, it was time to visit the new local venue, Sofi Stadium.

Sean, Taylor, Cheesehead Sue, Kurth at Sofi Stadium

50th Anniversary of Moon Landing

Less than a month after we moved into Reatta Glen, we were on a plane to Houston. NASA had invited us to celebrate the 50th anniversary of the first lunar landing. At Space Center Houston, they put our image on the moon as if we were really there.

On the Moon with Armstrong and Aldrin

Sue had fun posing with a make believe astronaut just before they blasted off.

Sue with her Faux Astronaut at the 50th Anniversary of the Moon Landing

I was so disappointed that almost all the NASA people I worked with had died. I had forgotten that they were all older than I. But our friends, Charlie and Dotty Duke sat at our table for the festivities that night and helped us celebrate. Of the twelve that walked on the moon, only four were still alive. Charlie was the youngest. After dinner, Apollo 17 geologist astronaut Jack Schmitt and Apollo 13 lunar module pilot Fred Haise spent some time at our table reminiscing.

The next day, NASA bussed us over to the Mission Operations Control Room. They had brought the MOCR out of mothballs and restored it exactly to its condition at the time of the Apollo 11 landing July 20, 1969, even to the extent of the cigarette butts in the ashtrays.

In the Mission Operations Control Room Reenacting Apollo 11 Moon Landing

They had us sit in the VIP viewing area as they replayed the exciting 13 minute audio of the lunar module's powered landing on that historic day. It was nostalgic! This was the first time that Sue had been at Mission Control and reenacted the landing. Charlie had been the Apollo 11 Capsule Communicator in the MOCR, so we heard his famous words in response to Armstrong's, "The Eagle has landed.": "Thanks a lot, Eagle. You've got a bunch of guys turning blue here." One can hear this playback today at the Smithsonian Air and Space museum in Washington DC.

The next morning, we all posed for a picture at the Hilton Hotel.

Dotty, Charlie, Sue, Kurth

Special Anniversaries

Scott and Sheryl gave us a surprise evening for our 25th wedding anniversary. We were picked up in a limousine and taken to one of our favorite restaurants.

But they surpassed us for our 40th anniversary. We returned hoine from playing golf to find.more than 40 of our friends yelling "Surprise!" Sheryl had swiped our Christmas list and invited everyone.The backyard was full of people, balloons, and a bar manned by our favorite Mesa Verde bartender. They presented us with fresh flowered leis and a cake.

Surprise 40th Wedding Anniversary Party

So Much Better than Cake,

We celebrated Sue's 80th birthday at Sheryl's home with some zany relatives. We may have had too much Champagne. Bob and Liisa are Sean's parents. Maureen Shroeder is Sean's sister. Michael is Maureen's husband. Silver is Taylor's husband. This fun-loving group not only gets together on these special occasions, but also on holidays.

Back row: Bob Gildea, Kurth. Sue, Maureen Shroeder, Liisa Gildea, Michael Schroeder, Sean. Front row: Griffin, Taylor, Silver Odish

We celebrated our 60th wedding anniversary at Reata Glen in 2023 with champagne. The family turned out in force.

Our 60th wedding anniversary was even better at home.

Another Very Happy Occasion with My Soul Mate

2. The Occupational Therapist

Sue began her year of internship, required for Occupational Therapy certification, at three different hospitals around the country, while I attended graduate school at Wisconsin in September 1962. She began at Mary Free Bed Rehabilitation Hospital in Cleveland, Ohio. Four months later she interned in Grand Rapids, Michigan. Her final assignment was in Milwaukee 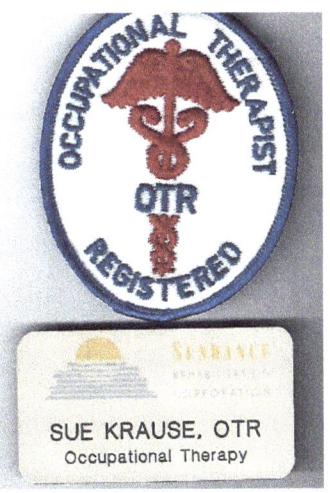 County Hospital. At that point She became a Registered Occupational Therapist. I was so proud of her. After her residency, Sue accepted a permanent position at Milwaukee County Hospital to apply her new skills as an OTR in a new pilot program in psychiatry. Sue proudly displayed her OTR credentials on her uniform. The role was challenging, even though two psychologists were assigned to the program full time.

Sue dealt with two groups of mentally ill children: one was pre-teen; the other was teenagers. She learned to deal with the physically aggressive ones by earning their respect and showing no fear. One ten-year old liked to throw a baseball at her as hard as he could, but she caught the ball and returned it to him. (The sports skills taught by her father paid off once again.) Another large 16-year old female attacked Sue from behind in the corridor, but she was able to talk her out of life-threatening violence.

Sue worked diligently and effectively in her profession until she become pregnant in 1964. She was reluctant to leave the profession she loved, but she was anxious to become a full tine stay-at-home mom. But she did not return to OT for almost 30 years. My earnings were sufficient to support us. Sue found important pursuits outside the profession that utilized her special talent. Nevertheless, she kept her credentials current in case we needed her earnings. Frequently she did receive solicitations from recruiters because OTs were in high demand.

In January 1993 I lost my job. My company continued paying me until I found a new position, but we were not sure how long that would last. It was a terrible time in the aerospace industry. I spent months searching for a new job and a comparable salary. We did not want to move. Sue thought we could survive on our savings until I convinced her that we could not without significantly compromising our lifestyle. So, she stepped up to the challenge.

She took a refresher course in occupational therapy and contacted the recruiters. She was surprised at the size of the offers. It was as if she had never left the profession. The need of OTRs in the rehabilitation segment of the profession was high. The offers in 1993 were almost $50 per hour. She learned the company was billing her out at $250 per hour. But the billable hours required hands-on care. Neither breaks nor the time to generate the required paperwork were billable hours. Therefore, she was under great pressure to provide as much hands-on service as possible. She excelled almost immediately. Management loved the maturity and work ethic of this middle-aged superstar. The company even wanted her to open a new office in Studio City. But this meant a commute of more than 50 miles through LA traffic. She agreed to open the office and get it started. But the commute was grueling. So, after four weeks, she turned down the promotion to manage it permanently. She returned to the local office in Costa Mesa

Sue enjoyed treating the elderly patients as long as she saw progress. But management pressured her to maximize her billable hours by treating patients who were unresponsive. She refused, stating she had to protect her credential license. At this time, I had found a high-paying job, and we did not need the extra money. When she came home and complained about the unethical pressure, I suggested she resign. Her eyes lit up, and she gave me her classic big smile. She went directly to her typewriter and wrote her letter of resignation. I was proud of her.

3. The Mother

In 1964, our second year of marriage, we decided it was time to begin expanding our family. Sue wanted two children; I wanted four. Soon she became pregnant. So, we bought our first home, a model in New Berlin, a Milwaukee suburb, using the money we saved from Sue's salary as a down payment. As soon as we moved in December 1964, Sue began decorating the nursery. She painted colorful giant blocks, balls, and animals on the walls and ceiling, demonstrating her artistic and motherly skills. In the spring she resigned her job as an occupational therapist to prepare to become a stay-at-home mom. She proved to be an outstanding maternity patient, rigorously following the doctor's advice to exercise in preparation for the birth. Scott Alan Krause was born

June 9, 1965, in less than three hours of labor; seven pounds, three ounces, 21 inches. Both Sue and Scott were healthy. I was a very proud papa. Sue even looked pretty immediately after childbirth. Once again, Sue declared we would have only two children in order to give them all the love, attention, and affordability required for a full childhood. I compromised and set my sights on three children.

But just three months later we moved to Boston. I accepted an offer to join the staff at the Instrumentation Lab at the Massachusetts Institute of Technology in Cambridge responsible for designing the flight software for the Apollo mission. We rented out our New Berlin home to three bachelors, who were colleagues at GM. Baby Scott only got to enjoy his specially decorated nursery for three months. Our parents were going to miss us, so we promised to return each Christmas enabling them to watch Scott grow.

Soon after we arrived in Boston, we went to famous Durgin Park for lunch. We were told we could bypass the long lines to get in by first stopping for a drink at the downstairs pub. They would then give us a ticket to go directly upstairs for lunch. But when Sue put baby Scott lying in his basinet on the bar, the proprietor informed us that Scott was too young to be on the bar.

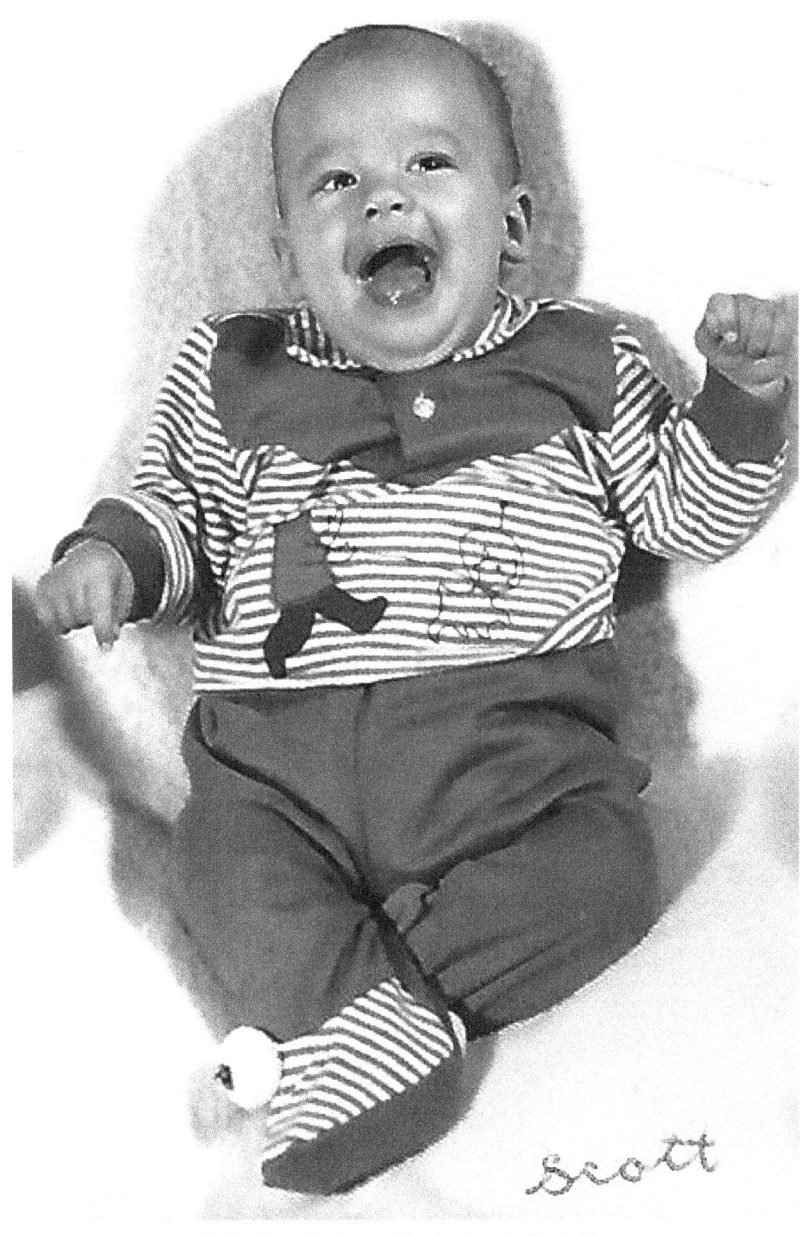

Baby Scott Underage On the Durgin Park Bar

We moved into a small rental home on Boston's North Shore in Danvers. But try as she did to get acquainted, the neighbors were not friendly; none had children as young as Scott. After six months the neighbors next door invited us over to meet the other neighbors. The one that greeted us at the door asked from where we had moved. He responded he had never heard of Milwaukee! When I told him it was 90 miles north of Chicago, he said, "Oh yes; that's out near California somewhere."

Sue was happy to take Scott everywhere while we explored the beauty and wonders of New England. We took many weekend car trips throughout Massachusetts, New Hampshire, Vermont, and Connecticut. Scott was a great baby and seemed to enjoy the travel.

Sue and I looked forward to expanding our taste for frozen rock lobster tails that we had acquired in Wisconsin. We thought we would take advantage of the plentiful Maine lobsters offered in the Boston area, but we learned the fish markets did not offer frozen lobster – instead, only live ones! So, Sue bought two live lobsters and tried to prepare them. She tried to force them into a pot of boiling water, but they screamed and began to climb out of the pot. In frustration, she grabbed them and threw them into the freezer. She succeeded in killing them, but the meat was spoiled. Thereafter we only had lobster at restaurants.

Sue got pregnant again during our second year in Massachusetts after we moved to a larger rental home in West Peabody, north of Cambridge. Although the 18 mile commute was still a challenge, the neighborhood was much better. Sue made lifelong friends with our next-door neighbors, Nancy and Bill King. Their kids were a bit older than Scott, but now he had playmates.

The trilevel home at the top of a hill was perfect for parties, although the winter snow crept into our family room. It was here that I learned how Sue loved theme parties. In my opinion, they were over the top, but our neighbors loved them.

Blondie and Her Toga Party

Our precious second child, Sheryl Lynn Krause was born in Lynn, Massachusetts on March 31, 1967. My sister and her husband were visiting us, when Sue announced it was time to get to the hospital. Sue was hardly showing; the nurses asked why she was there. They would not let me into the delivery room (old-fashioned custom), so I proceeded to drop off our guests at the airport, expecting many hours of labor. But Sheryl was already born when I returned. I learned that Sue was furious with the obstetrician when he refused to give her a spinal block because she had a pilonidal cyst that he had not discovered earlier. So, she had to deliver with nothing to mitigate the pain. It was fortunate that Sheryl was born in just 45 minutes, weighing five pounds 15 ounces and only 19 inches long. Both were quite healthy when I was

Scott Fascinated with Baby Sheryl

allowed to see them. Sheryl was a beautiful baby and Sue continued to be as pretty as ever. Scott and I were so proud.

Scott was so proud of his baby sister.

Sue still wanted only two children. I compromised and settled on two. She was now a busy mother with two in diapers. She was so happy that our family was now complete.

My work on the Apollo flight software was completed in September, so it was time to return to the GM aerospace plant in Milwaukee and reoccupy our home in New Berlin. MIT offered me a permanent role to remain on the Instrumentation staff with a 10% salary increase, but we turned it down. I had also interviewed other companies with better offers. We ultimately accepted a 25% increase with TRW requiring a move to Houston Texas to support the Apollo missions. Sue was once again overjoyed with our adventure of change – four moves in four years!

As Sheryl grew, her love for Sue knew no bounds.

But Sue would tell you that our kids were not always perfect. One day, she called me at work telling me to rush home because "I'm gonna kill the kid!" Scott had locked himself in his room with a can of spray paint. He proceeded to spray-paint the walls, the carpeting, even his clothes inside his drawers.

Sue decided the kids needed a pet. She bought a little Peekapoo puppy and named it Melissa. She trained it to stay off the family room carpet and walk around its outside on the bare floor. After it grew to adulthood (five pounds), she decided to educate the kids. She mated it with a toy poodle. It produced five adorable puppies, which she sold to the neighborhood kids for $35 each. Although our neighbors weren't too happy about it, they couldn't resist their children's pleas.

When the kids were old enough to attend school, Sue taught art at St. Thomas in Nassau Bay Texas. Scott and

Sheryl were so proud of their mom, the teacher. Sue raised Scott and Sheryl into happy, self-confident kids.

She took them to the community pool in El Lago almost daily. They both became accomplished swimmers competing for ribbons. Sue attended all their swim meets. She gave the kids packets of Jello crystals for quick energy. They wore their bright-colored fingers as a badge of honor.

Sheryl was particularly proud of her ribbons. She displayed them on her bulletin board in her room under a banner that read: "Sheryl the Greatest." Sue became a den mother for Scott's Cub Scout troop. Sheryl and I participated in Indian Princesses. Sue always loved making the kids feel special with their birthday parties.

Special Birthday Parties

Scott's Fifth Birthday

Sue was also a warrior when it came time to defend her kids. She discovered one of the four poisonous Texas snakes in our backyard, a copperhead. No problem. She grabbed a shovel and beat it to death.

When we moved to California in time for the kids to start the new school year, Sue was happy to learn that the Newport/Mesa School district was one of the best in the state. They were coming from the best local school in Texas. The melting pot of astronaut families coming together from all over the country enabled a diverse opportunity to learn. As a result, they were receiving a great education in El Lago. But Sue closely monitored their Costa Mesa curriculum and was disappointed. They were not learning anything new. The classes were just a review of what they had learned in Texas. She requested a meeting with the Costa Mesa teachers and presented them with a four-page newspaper that Scott had created the previous school year. It had sections of news, sports, weather, and entertainment. But the teachers declared they could never ask their students to undertake such a challenge.

When we moved to California, Sue bought a kitten for the kids and named it Missy. It was black and white with markings that resembled a skunk. Sue trained it to be an outside cat. Missy like to share her meals with a local skunk that visited our backyard. Either Missy thought she was a skunk, or the skunk thought Missy was a relative.

Under Sue's guidance, both excelled in high school academics and extracurricular activities. For music, Scott first tried Sue's childhood flute, then graduated to saxophone. He borrowed the money from Sheryl to buy a guitar. Eventually, he became the drum major for the marching band. Sheryl was a cheerleader and became the costumed mascot for the football team. Sue encouraged her to also join the Choc-ettes, a girls' club supporting fund raising for Children's Hospital of Orange County.

Both kids became good golfers. Scott was the team captain; Sheryl played on the boys' team because their high school did not have a girls' team. Sheryl was elected Prom Queen her junior year. Both continued to do well academically: Scott due to his extraordinarily high IQ, Sheryl because she was driven and worked extremely hard. She wanted to be a teacher like her mom and needed good grades to be accepted into a good college that offered a solid teaching curriculum.

Happy Wife, Happy Life

Both had high aspirations for college. Sue encouraged Scott to obtain appointments to West Point and the Air Force Academy. Sue proved with phonographs that Scott did not have scoliosis as erroneously reported by the Army physician. Then she helped him add the pounds required by Air Force Academy admission standards by feeding him rich chocolate shakes daily. Sheryl was admitted to her first choice, Cal Poly San Luis Obispo, by authoring an insightful essay on why she wanted to become a teacher.

Getting Ready for Empty Nest

Scott graduated from the USAF Academy as a distinguished graduate in 1987. Sue's and my parents all attended the ceremony at Falcon Stadium in Colorado Springs. We videotaped the entire program. Scott was accepted into pilot training at Williams AFB and began a 20 year career as an Air Force pilot. Immediately after graduation, he began a quest to find a mate. Six months later he married Pam DeKonty from Pheonix. Pam earned her degree in finance from Arizona State.

Sheryl joined the Alpha Chi Omega Sorority. She was accepted into the highly-sought Cal Poly teaching program her junior year. She graduated in 1989.

Sheryl announced her engagement to Sean Gildea, who graduated from Cal State Santa Barbara. She planned to stay at home for one year before they married to begin a nest egg. She became a third-grade teacher in the Huntington Beach school system, acquiring the job because could speak Spanish fluently, a requirement due to the Spanish-speaking children and parents. She taught her lessons in both languages. Sheryl taught second and third grade for nine years. Today she is the regional sales manager for Oceanside Glass Tile, the company founded by husband Sean.

Sue set up the rules for Sheryl to live at home for the one year before her marriage. Sheryl accepted these rules gracefully. But Sue was overjoyed to help her plan the wedding. Initially Sheryl did not want the reception at Mesa Verde CC because some of her friends had held it there. But after Sue helped her explore alternatives, Sheryl agreed with our favorite venue. The wedding at our church, St. Andrews in Newport Beach, and the reception were some of the most joyous occasions, not only for the wedding couple and their guests, but for Sue and me as well.

The empty nest filled us with mixed emotions. We were proud our children had begun their adult lives with happiness and self-esteem for their own futures with their wonderful spouses, but we were also saddened to cut the apron strings.

But we did experience trauma after Scott retired from the Air Force and continued his meteoric career climb. His first foray into the political sector began as the Chief of Staff for Management under President Bush in the Department of Homeland Security. Later, after joining the Trump transition team, he was appointed DHS Executive Secretary under President Trump. In the private business sector, he became a director with Deloitte Touche, later a director with Cisco Systems. Less than one week after he and I won the Mesa Verde annual Derby golf tournament, and he returned to Virginia; he suffered a massive stroke. His chiropractor, during a neck adjustment, had severed a blood vessel to his brain.

Sue and I flew to the local Virginia hospital where he had been admitted. Sue researched and found a better hospital in Washington DC and, with Pam's permission, had him transferred. Scott was completely paralyzed on his right side. He was blind in his right eye and could not talk. Sue worked with him and, with the help of a speech therapist, gradually taught him the alphabet and several words. The physical therapist and occupational therapist were also wonderful. The doctor told us he would regain all his mental acuity, but not his physical ability. But Scott was healthy, highly motivated, and still young at age 47. As a result, he recovered almost 100% after a year of therapy. The doctors wanted to fit him for a mechanical aid for walking, but he refused. We were once again so very proud of him.

Later, Scott earned his broker's license in Virginia and teamed up with Pam as a real estate agent in Washington DC, Virginia, and Maryland.

Loving Son

Loving Daughter

4. The Artist

Sue always had a talent for art. In addition to her Occupational Therapy major, she minored in art at the University of Wisconsin, inspired by realist painter and printmaker Aaron Bohrod. There she created works in several media: watercolors, oils, acrylics, sculpture, hooked rugs, and mosaic tile.

When our children began school in Texas, she found time to begin an art career in earnest. She sold some of her first pen and ink drawings, watercolors, and acrylics to friends and neighbors; some were commissioned. She hosted several successful local one-women shows. Sue served as president of the Clear Creek Art League from 1977 to 1980, and she received an honorary lifetime membership.

But it wasn't until she attended the Houston Museum of Fine Art that she really found her niche under the tutelage of well-known artist Earl Staley. He told her to use her talent with pen and ink line drawings to become an etcher. He informed her that Rembrandt was one of the first etchers. Sue respected Staley and took his advice, which led her to an amazingly successful career. She took classes from Staley for many months, using his personal etching press, before we moved to California. There she continued her education at the Laguna School of Art in Laguna Beach.

Sue's etchings were always hand-pulled, limited editions; never more than 75 numbered originals plus artist proofs. As she acquired more experience, her etchings became unique and exceptional. They were mostly scenes of nature, windmills, animals, and Navaho Indians weaving their baskets. But Sue carved her zinc plates into features of the scene and set the plates into matboard. Usually, the matboard itself was a template for embossments. She would ink the plates by hand and pull the complete collage through the etching press. Often, she water-colored each image after it came off the press.

We had to enlarge one bedroom by an additional 200 square feet to enable room for the huge etching press. She also had to install a heavy-duty fan, sink, and large worktables in her studio. She acquired a small portable press to enable demonstration of her skill as she traveled to galleries.

In 1982, the prestigious Southwest Art magazine commissioned Sue to publish a four page article to show how she created her embossed etchings as shown below. Her fame was growing.

Reprinted from Southwest Art Magazine • February, 1982 • Volume 11, No. 9

THE ART OF INTAGLIO PRINTING

by Sue Krause

Sue Krause, THE WEAVER - SURVIVOR OF TIME, etching/embossing with hand coloring, Arches Cover, 30 x 22, Edition: 75

As long as I can remember, I've admired the design qualities of Navajo rugs and the dedicated women who weave them. I decided to create a Navajo weaver image using the rug pattern on the loom as the influence for the plate shape and the embossed design. After numerous drawings of Indian women engaged in weaving activities with backgrounds and children, I used tracing paper to arrange the figures and to come up with a final composition. Using colored pencils I worked out the colors that would later be painted on the etched and inked portion of the image.

Creating the etching begins with transferring the plate shape outlined on the drawing onto Arches Cover paper, making sure that the drawing is smaller than the rectangular 15-gauge zinc plate that I will be using. The paper is taped onto the top of the metal plate, and the basic plate shape is cut out with a saber saw. The rag paper combines with the metal keeping it cool and allowing the saw to cut smoothly. Intricate shapes are achieved by using a coping saw (fig. 1).

Southwest Art

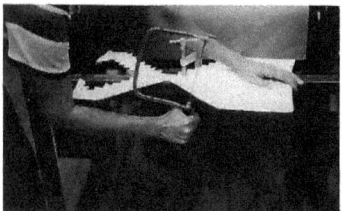

1. Cutting the plate

2. Filing the edges of the plate

3. Polishing the plate

After cutting the plate, the edges are filed and slightly beveled (fig. 2) preventing rough edges which can hold unwanted ink. Using Putz Pomade, the zinc plate is coated and hand rubbed, polishing it to mirror reflection. The plate must be completely pit free in order to achieve the pure whites (fig. 3).

When the pomade is removed, the plate is washed and placed on a hotplate and a ground of wax and asphaltum acid resist is applied. In this case, two types of ground will be used: first, the plate will be coated with a soft-ball greasy ground distributed with a brayer (fig. 4-5). When the ground has cooled the plate is placed on the press bed. Fabric is then laid over the ground side of the plate, with a sheet of wax paper and the press blanket to follow. Turning the press wheel will force the plate and its coverings through the press and cause the fabric texture to be imprinted into the soft ground (fig. 6). Before placing the plate in the nitric acid solution to etch the texture, the areas where the line drawing exists will be covered with asphaltum or a total acid resist which allows no etching in those areas. The texture is to be etched lightly at the top of the plate, with darkening around the lower edges. Consequently, the plate will be initially put into the nitric acid solution for five minutes. The plate is then rinsed with water, dried and liquid resist applied to areas requiring a light etch. The plate continues to be immersed in the acid, cleaned, and the resist applied until the desired line depth is achieved.

4. Applying the ground

5. Distributing the ground

6. Imprinting the fabric texture

Now the soft ground is removed with paint thinner and the hard-ball ground is applied using heat and a brayer, leaving a smooth light brown surface on the plate. After the plate has cooled, the soft pencil drawing on paper is placed face down on the hard-ground surface and gently pulled through the press, transferring a mirror image of the pencil drawing to the plate. These pencil lines serve as the guidelines for drawing the image with a stylus that just breaks the surface of the ground. Areas not to be etched are again covered with asphaltum, and once again the plate is immersed into the acid. A feather is used to wipe away the bubbles during the reaction, thus slowing it down and creating an even bite or etching of the plate. Again the immersion time is regulated with frequent returns to the acid bath to increase depth of line.

Now that the line work or intaglio is created, a proof is run. The plate is inked, wiped, and printed on the paper to be used in the edition. Further printing details will be explained when the image is completed. After examining the first proof, a soft pencil is used to render the values in the image. Using a scale from 0 - 10 to indicate shades, 0 being white and 10 being darkest, the plate is prepared for the aquatint process.

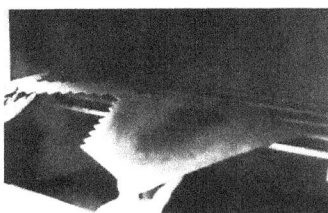

7. *Placing plate into rosin box*

8. *Dipping into acid bath*

Aquatinting begins when the clean plate, etched and polished, is placed on a dowel shelf in a rosin box *(fig. 7)* with plenty of powdered rosin (another acid resist) on the bottom; the door is closed and a bellows is placed in a hole at the level of the rosin. The rosin is blown evenly onto the plate and allowed to settle. The plate is then gingerly moved to the hotplate where the heat melts the rosin particles creating droplets of resist. After cooling the plate, a liquid resist is painted on all of the areas to be left pure white (0 on the drawing). The plate is then immersed in acid for only a second to create the first (or number 1 on the scale) shade, then it is rinsed with water *(fig. 8)*, dried, and all areas marked with the first (1) shade covered with resist. This process continues at five and ten second intervals until the final or darkest (10) remains. The etching time is about five minutes to achieve the darkest darks.

The plate is once again cleaned, inked, and readied for another proof. If the results of the aquatint or shading appear too dark, a burnisher may be used to fold the metal back into the lines. If too light the aquatint process must be completed again, first painting with resist the areas which are satisfactory. Proofs and adjustments continue until the image reaches the desired state.

Now the plate shape is incorporated with the embossment template. The embossment is created by using three mat boards totaling the size and shape of the image. The pattern is drawn with a white pencil and then carved with an X-acto knife *(fig. 9)*. The template is then waterproofed with coats of lacquer.

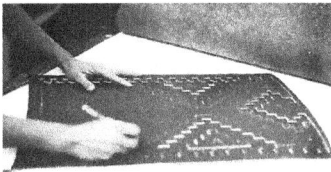

9. *Cutting embossment in template*

10. *Applying ink*

Arches Cover (100 percent rag paper) is soaked in water for about an hour to allow it to accept ink and stretch for the embossment.

Printing of the etching plate begins with warming the plate on a hotplate and applying the raw umber, oil-based etching ink with a small piece of mat board *(fig. 10)*. The ink is forced into the lines, and at this point, completely covers the plate. The excess ink is then removed with a tarlatan (cheese cloth with starch), trying not to pull ink from the lines *(fig. 11)*.

11. Wiping away excess ink

12. Handwiping the plate

13. Positioning the plate on the template

The remaining surface ink is removed by handwiping *(fig. 12)*. All areas to be white are polished with small pieces of the rag paper. The edges of the plate are cleaned with a towel.

With the plate in place, the template is put on the bed of the press *(fig. 13)*. The paper is then removed from the water, blotted and placed over the template. A special layer of foam rubber is laid on the paper and then the press blankets are applied on top. The correct press pressure is set and the wheel turned to force the plates through the press to produce the embossment *(fig. 14)*. The blankets are then lifted and the paper removed to a drying board and stapled flat. The plate is cleaned with paint thinner in a tub of sawdust and made ready for the next print *(fig. 15)*. Each time an image is printed, the inking and wiping procedures are repeated.

When the print is dry, it is hand-watercolored, titled and given an edition number. Original prints are printed and numbered in sequence with the edition amount determined before printing begins. One tenth of the edition number can be artist proofs which are printed before the edition numbering begins. This image, THE WEAVER — SURVIVOR OF TIME, will be an edition of 75 prints. Once the complete edition is printed, the plate will be cancelled with an etched "X." ■

14. Pulling the print

15. Cleaning the plate

Sue juried into several art shows. We had to take her work on the plane when she juried into the Lakefront Festival of Arts in 1978 at the Milwaukee Art Center. Sales began well until a cloudburst forced us to pack up and abandon the show. Undaunted, she contacted a Milwaukee downtown gallery. The owner bought all her remaining etchings! I was relieved that we would not have to lug them back on the plane home. She also displayed her etchings in the summer show in Phoenix,

Sue displayed her work in the Beverly Hills annual show for several years. Again, the sales were good. But her most prolific shows were the all-juried shows each summer at the Art-A-Fair in Laguna Beach. They restricted allowing only 20% of the artists to come from Laguna Beach non-residents.

Sue eventually was asked to be President and General Manager of Art-A-Fair on the year they moved further southwest down Canyon Road in Laguna. Sue had to preside over building the infrastructure at this new location. The organization faced several challenges: First, they had to solicit the approval of the Laguna Beach Design and Review Committee, which had a reputation for rejecting any project which might infringe on the traditions of the city. Sue enlisted a member of her own committee to attend the meeting to record the session. This recording captured the arrogance and discourtesy of the D&R members as they voted to disallow the proposed construction. Sue presented this evidence to the Laguna Beach City Council who then overturned the decision. She proved to be a tough, determined, and persistent leader.

Next, she had to hire contractors for the construction, but ran out of money. The organization was in such a crisis that I suggested she file Chapter 7 (not 11) bankruptcy on behalf of Art-A-Fair. Instead, she met with each lien holder and negotiated a long-term payment schedule. She successfully used the argument that they could insist on payment now, forcing the organization to declare bankruptcy, or they could eventually be paid for their services by accepting her deferred payment terms. They all accepted!

Her final challenge was to survive a test by the fire department to withstand the weight of a fully loaded firetruck on the newly constructed concrete culvert from the road to their site. It passed and they were in business. The members awarded Sue a lifetime membership in Art-A-Fair, which is thriving to this day.

But Sue was also an art collector. The first time we toured New Orleans, Sue was enthralled, visiting almost every gallery in town. We found one that featured Salvador Dali's striking suite of thirteen lithographs, his Alice in Wonderland assemblage. They were amazing, many featuring melting clocks. Sue knew they could be valuable someday. The current price was $250 for each or the entire suite for $3,000. One issue was how to display and preserve them, as they were large and delicate. After several visits to the gallery, we decided not to buy them. Instead, we bought an impressive watercolor of a jazz band of musicians by German artist Leo Meiersdorff. Twenty years later after Dali died, the Alice in Wonderland edition was advertised for one million dollars. (I Wish I had listen to her.)

When the Wrigley Mansion in Santa Catilina was leased by a group who converted it to a bed and breakfast, they hired Sue to create four etchings of the complex to hang in the Mansion. They picked her up in a helicopter and flew her to the island. She created an edition of 75. The artist's proofs are still hanging in the mansion today. The main one is shown below.

Sue Krause

1918 Suva Circle   Costa Mesa, California 92626   (714) 545-4354

BIRTH: February 25, 1940, in Fond du Lac, Wisconsin
EDUCATION: B.S., University of Wisconsin, Madison; Houston Museum of Fine Art School; The Art Institute of Southern California; Orange Coast College and Golden West College.
GALLERIES: Haggenmaker Galleries, Laguna Beach, CA, (714) 494-2675; Trailside Galleries, Jackson Hole, WY, (307) 733-3186; Stebbins Gallery, Kemah, TX, (713) 334-5711; Ann Conner Gallery, Appleton, WI, (414) 733-7420; Wenniger Graphics, Boston, (617) 536-4688; Ken Dew Gallery, Huntington Beach, CA, (714) 968-6040.

COMMISSIONS: Price depending on size of image and edition.
SUBJECT MATTER: Landscapes, florals, beachscapes, westerns
MEDIUM: Etchings-hand-colored and embossed, watercolor.
LIMITED EDITION PRINTS: No, all originals.
ARTIST COMMENTS: My etchings are a composite of favorite places where I've lived or visited. Each time I try to save a warm memory.
MAJOR INFLUENCES: Evelyn Stebbins, Bob Camblin and all the people enjoying and recalling the same scenes I have recreated.

"The Inn on Mt. Ada"   18 x 24   Hand-colored Etching   Ed. of 75

Sue secured a perpetual display of her etchings in Haggenmaker Gallery in Laguna Beach:

Her Personal Corner of the Haggenmaker Gallery in Newport Beach

Ultimately, she was featured in 18 galleries across the country. In addition to the Laguna Beach galleries: Haggenmaker, The Back Door Gallery, and Petricks, she was featured in Trailside in Jackson Hole WY, Stebbins in Kemah TX, Ann Conor in Appleton WI, Wenniger Graphics in Boston, Longpre in La Canada-Flintridge CA, MGM Grand Gallery in Las Vegas, Copenhagen in Solvang CA, Peabody's, Inc. in Fond du Lac WI, Designs Recycled in Fullerton CA, Popes Collectors in Charlotte NC, Kight in Long Beach, Bergstrom's Art Center in Neenah WI, Holloway in San Clemente CA, David Barnett in Milwaukee, and Ken Dew in Huntington Beach CA.

Some of her collectors owned more than twenty of her creations.

Her early acrylic work was also acclaimed, but she abandoned these for etchings as suggested by her mentors.

Showing Off Her Earliest Work

This is a display of some of her largest etchings of which she sold the entire edition of 75.

Harbor in View

Calm in the Afternoon

Oak Meadows

Ready for Harvest

Windmill County

Despite her roaring success, she remained humble. This is the self-portrait she displayed in her studio. So funny!

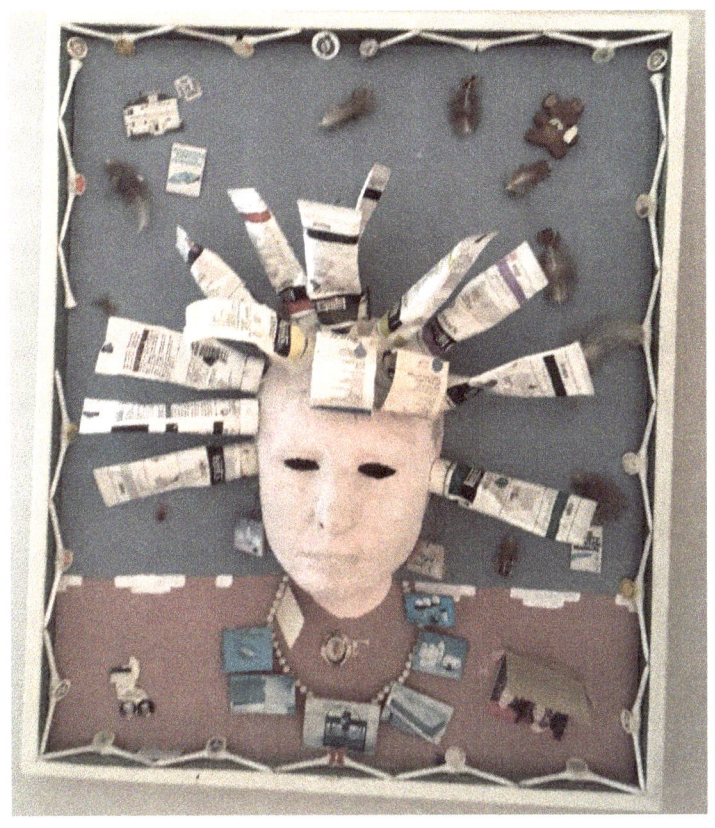

Sue's Self Portrait Depicting Her Multifaceted Life

Sue vigorously protected the quality and integrity of her work. All of her etchings were fair-traded (She allowed none of her galleries to reduce the price she set for each edition.) Each etching sold in her galleries were accompanied by a certificate of authenticity, signed by Sue. The one exception occurred when they were sold on secondary market for which she had no control of the price. But these were listed at a higher price.

On one occasion she discontinued her relationship with a gallery which she concluded was unethical. The MGM gallery in Las Vegas did a great business, typically selling 10-12 of her pieces every quarter for three years. We arrived one day with ten new etchings. They had sold all but one of the previous consignment. But a new saleswoman greeted us. She told a pair of gallery customers that they could negotiate with Sue on the remaining piece. Without saying a word, Sue picked up the piece and walked out of the gallery in a huff, never to return. Three weeks later the MGM experienced their famous fire. All the artwork in the gallery was destroyed and not covered by insurance.

5. The Philanthropist

No, we were not wealthy; we did not have millions to donate. But Sue was a philanthropist, nevertheless. When we moved to California in 1975, she joined the Costa Mesa guild of the Children's Hospital of Orange County (CHOC). She quickly became active in their fundraisers. Below shows us attending one that was held at the Center Club in Costa Mesa.

Sue at the Center Club Fund Raiser

She became the Program Chairman for the annual Bear Review, a variety show staring local performers to raise money for CHOC. Her committee hired a professional director who brought the costumes, music, and skits. Sue also performed with two other women singing "Bad Boy Leroy Brown." During a commercial break, she tried to elegantly parade across the stage modeling a Nordstrom dress, but her balloons tangled with another woman crossing the opposite way. Undaunted, she continued to walk with her hand in the air, but without balloons. Sheryl was ushering at the time and almost rolled down the aisle with laughter.

Eventually, Sue was invited to join the Fashion Show Board of Children's Hospital of Orange County. Each year, the Board organizes a two day fashion show to raise money for CHOC. Sue donated her time and money annually to make the event a huge success. After serving for several years, Sue was chosen to be the general chairman in 1992.

Her theme was Viva La France. Sue loved themes and enjoyed going over the top. She hired the professional models to strut their stuff down the elevated red carpet. She recruited I. Magnin to provide the 141 dresses, gowns, suits, bathing suits, jeans, blouses, slacks, and jackets of the Karl Lagerfeld Spring Collection that the models displayed on the runway. Designers included Oscar de la Renta, Yves Saint Laurant, Calvin Klein, Armani, Valentino, Dior, Perry Elis, St. Johns, Ferragamo, Ann Klein, Chanel, and Bob Mackie. She recruited a professional producer, a director, and an accomplished master of ceremonies, and she hired a great band for the entertainment. This was the program for the finale.

The event was a huge success. Sue's committee bought her the red St. Johns suit up for auction when she failed to get the winning bid. The next year the guild honored her in an extraordinary way:

Punch and Judy Guild Salutes Sue Krause As Our WOMAN OF THREE DECADES!

As a member of Punch and Judy since moving to California in 1975, Sue has served as Guild President, has been a member of the Fashion Show Advisory Boards of 1985-1993, 1996 - 2002 and as Chairman of the 1992 "Vive La France" Fashion Show, as well as playing a very active role in and frequent hostess of our many social functions. Thank you, Sue!

But Sue's philanthropy was not limited to Children's Hospital. In addition to St Andrews Church, she donated annually to the American Red Cross, Northeast of the Well, and the American Cancer Society.

She served on the El Lago Pool and Recreation Association and was named Parks Commissioner from 1972-74. She served on the Costa Mesa Board of Tourism, Arts, and Promotion in 1989-90. Sue was a member of the Discovery Museum of Orange County from its founding in 1975. She was featured in the 18th Edition of Who's Who of American Women in 1994.

6. The Golfer

Sue's dad, Arnold Firle, was a champion amateur golfer, with a scratch handicap. He taught Sue at age 8, then turned her over to a professional for lessons at age 11. She became an accomplished player, winning junior tournaments in the state of Wisconsin as a teenager.

Teenage Champion

Arnie's family were members of the Fond du Lac South Hills Country Club. His whole family played golf regularly: her mother, Meta, and her sister, Sandy, in addition to Sue and Arnie. Sue and I followed her dad around the second 18 of a 36 hole final in South

Hill's club championship in 1964, which he won on the final hole at age 50; his fourth win. Sue was so proud of her dad who was not used to walking all 36 holes.

When we were dating, Sue invited me to play South Hills often. But Sue beat me every time until well after we were married. At age 28 we joined Baywood Country Club in South Texas. There I took lessons and eventually could play at Sue's level. She also played a mean game of tennis on Baywood's courts.

We joined Mesa Verde Country Club when we moved to Costa Mesa California in 1975. In addition to mentoring our children with their junior golf pursuits, Sue became a mainstay on the ladies' golf team. One year she was in the lead for the Ladies Club Championship but lost when her ball found the water on the final hole. (Tom Weiskopf also went into the water from the same tee when the PGA seniors played their tournament at MVCC.)

Our club hosted six LPGA tournaments in the 1980s. Sue opened our home to some of the younger players, and formed a lasting friendship with one, Nancy Scranton. Nancy invited us to all the LPGA tournaments she entered in California. She became a winner on the tour. Then in 1991 she won a major, the du Maurier Classic. Sue was thrilled for her.

Sue with Teammate Vanda Peterson at Mesa Verde Country Club

Sue scored her first hole-one-one on August 17, 2003, on the 12th hole at MVCC using a 9-wood, One year later she did it again from a different tee using a 5-iron, demonstrating it was no fluke.

Thanks to Sue's commitment, our kids became accomplished golfers. They both played organized junior golf. Sue transported them to all the tournaments in Southern California. Scott was the captain of his high school golf team and went on to play for the Air Force Academy for four years. Sheryl played on the boys' high school team for four years because the school did not have a girls' team. In 1982, Sheryl was the MVCC Junior Girls Champion. Sue inspired us to be a true golfing family.

A Golfing Family Not in Attire

In 1970, our family played on several of the famous Pinehurst golf courses in North Carolina. We took Sheryl to Hawaii in 1975 to celebrate her high school graduation and played at Mauna Lani on the big island. She shot 77! Sheryl now plays only once per year, but she has beaten her long-hitting husband every time they played together even though he plays more often.

Arizona Golfers

We enjoyed playing golf together as a family around the country until Sue's hip replacement and dislocation restricted her swing, causing her to give up the game after 70 years.

But Sue excelled in another sport in which her talent was unexpected: deep sea fishing. We were on a cruise in the

Seychelles Islands in the Indian Ocean. We were approached by two passengers who were looking for two others to share the cost of hiring a boat to take us deep sea fishing. Sue jumped at the opportunity. We hopped aboard and the captain and crew took us more than an hour away from the cruise ship deep into the Indian Ocean. The two other men and I caught nothing, but Sue caught eight fish. One was a beautiful dolphinfish, almost three feet long. After a ten minute fight, as she brought her catch alongside the boat, we marveled at the striking rainbow colors. But when she hoisted it into the boat, it turned grey and lost its beauty. Nevertheless, we were all looking forward to presenting it to the cruise chef for some wonderful mahi-mahi that night. But we were surprised when the captain deposited us on the cruise ship deck, then sped off with all of Sue's fish. We later learned that the captain was entitled to any fish we caught.

The next time we went deep sea fishing was in the Pacific Ocean off the California Coast. This time we were onboard with six other fishermen. But once again Sue caught eight fish and no one else snagged even one. We learned not to challenge the expert. She attributed her skill to freshwater fishing lessons from her dad.

7. The Cowgirl

Sue always had a love for horses and the desert. She dragged me to rodeos in Texas and California. She filled our homes with pictures of horses, cowgirl attire, and desert scenes. These are currently hanging on our walls.

Horses and Windmills Throughout Our Home

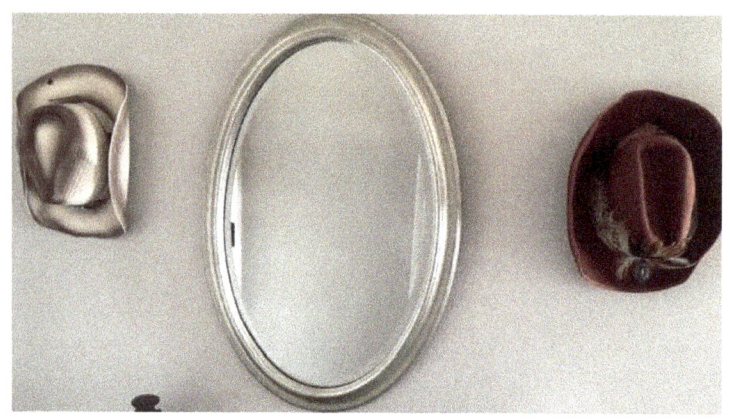

Sue's Favorite Headgear

Horses Everywhere!

Action Painting

Surrounded by Western Motif

She also loved horse races. We began to attend the quarter horse races in Los Alamitos. They were boring for me, but not for Sue. She signed up for every excursion from MVCC to attend the Del Mar races in San Diego. When we were visited by my brother Kirby, they would each put up one dollar for the two dollar bets at the track. They never won, but that didn't detract from their entertainment.

One day when we were vacationing in the El Conquistador golf resort in Puerto Rico, Sue insisted on leaving this beautiful paradise to travel 40 miles on poor roads in hot, humid weather to attend the horse races in San Juan on the other end of the island. I learned that the Hipódromo Camarero track "take" was much higher than the 17% seized by the proprietors on the US horse racetracks. We arrived early enough for Sue to venture down to the track to scientifically look over all the horses. After careful study, she knew exactly how to pick the winners for each race. She did. Every one of her eight picks finished dead last, except one — he finished second last. When we told the taxi driver on the way back, he could not stop laughing, claiming that had to be a record.

Happy Westerners

She loved the Tonto National Forest in Scottsdale Arizona which borders the Fort Apache Indian Reservation. When we moved to Southern California in 1975, she wanted to drive to the desert every year. Then we discovered the perfect dude ranch called Rancho De Los Caballeros among the Saguaro cactus in Wickenburg Arizona.

It offered 99 horses, a great golf course, and a full service spa. They had hayrides and campfire activities after dinner. Sue loved the country-western music they played every night. She was in her element.

After we spent several visits in the resort casitas with our friends, Sue decided it would be a perfect setting to celebrate our 45th anniversary with the family. She was concerned that we might not make it to our 50.th

Scott, Pam, Rachel, Griffin, Sean, Taylor, Sue, Karissa

She wanted to do it right. It worked perfectly because each of us were able to do the things we wanted. Sue, Scott, Sean, Sheryl and I played golf twice. Pam, Karissa, and Rachel had a massage at the spa. We all rode horses at least once. Griffin enjoyed the pool. Sue and Griffin went on their own horseback ride together. Sue learned how to gallop. One night someone brought out a telescope and we all looked at the moon, Jupiter, and Saturn. Then we went on a hayride to a barbeque.

45th Anniversary: Sean, Scott, Karissa, Pam, Rachel, Kurth, Taylor, Sheryl, Griffin, Sue

8. The Christian

Sue accepted Christ years before I did. We both attended the Lutheran Church in Madison while at UW and sporadically attended church throughout our early adult life in Milwaukee, Boston, and Houston. But we were not devoted followers until after our children came to Christ in earnest in the 1980s. Sue became a faithful follower in 1987, when she joined St, Andrews Presbyterian. I was still searching, trying to reconcile my knowledge of science with the apparent conflicts in the Bible, especially the first chapter of Genesis. Sue became a deacon of the church after my retirement in 1999.

We decided to attend the two-year course offered by the church: the Bethel Series. We read the entire Bible, which helped to open my eyes, although I still have some reservations about the harsh depiction of an unforgiving, vengeful God in the Old Testament. Also, several books, such as "The Case for Christ" by Lee Stroble convinced me. I subsequently joined the church. This made Sue and our children incredibly happy.

Sue and I attended several weekend couple retreats at Forest Home in the mountains of Southern California sponsored by St. Andrews. This strengthened our ties to the church members. We met new people here and formed a church "small group" which met regularly to discuss Biblical topics.

Sue took her ordination and installation as a deacon to heart. She ministered to dozens of members of the congregation for over 20 years. Even after moving to Reata Glen, she remained a faithful deacon to two of the elderly constituents. She went to lunch with one nonagenarian, Ruth Lampe, more than once each month. Sue encouraged Ruth in countless ways inspiring her to be an evangelist in her own community. One day, Ruth called to tell Sue she "was dying." Sue challenged her, saying not only was she not dying, but God needed her to continue her evangelism. Ruth agreed and is continuing to minister to her neighbors to this day. Ruth and Sue loved and respected each other.

In 1999, Sue agreed to chair a new committee at St. Andrews called Four Score and More. It was originated to sponsor an annual luncheon to honor octogenarians who were members of the church. Sue poured herself into the role, making the event a highlight on the St. Andrews calendar. Each year she and her committee created a new, but incredibly ambitious theme. They elaborately decorated the large hall, hired entertainers, and sent out invitations to hundreds of eligible church members months in advance of the event. One of Sue's themes was "Around the World in 80 Years." She acquired a hot air balloon basket, stood in it dressed as a world traveler, and welcomed each attendee with appropriate travel greetings. Another theme was the Academy Awards. She rolled out a red carpet and greeted each attendee with a microphone, commenting on their magnificent attire.

Sue loved to enact her themes.

She had a great sense of humor and was not reticent to make fun of herself. Once she dressed as a clown with a red wig, painted face, giant shoes, a bulbous red nose, and a funny hat, all consistent with the circus theme of the party. They loved it! Sue chaired Four Score and More for almost 20 years. When she turned 80, she was invited to the event and publicly honored.

Sue also volunteered to support many funeral services at St. Andrews. She was always sought after and made herself available.

In January 2023, Sue had a unique experience which she only shared with me because no one would believe her or think she was hallucinating. She saw a vivid image of Jesus, standing directly in front of her in our home. She was not frightened but was moved. Neither she nor Jesus spoke. She stood in Jesus' presence for at least a minute. This encounter was unique and remained vivid in her memory. She was not sure what it meant.

Sue prayed for others every night.

9. The Home Decorator

Sue had a zeel for change in each of our homes. A few months after we bought our first home in Milwaukee in 1964, she used her artists skills to paint a mural on the walls and ceiling of the nursury before Scott was born. It consisted of animals, colorful blocks, and balls. It is ironic that when we rented out our home to three bachelors, each one that would occupied that bedroom/nursery left to get married to the girl he impregnanted. Could they have been inspired by the subject matter on the walls?

When we bought our house in Texas in 1967, which I thought was perfect, Sue decided to adorn the main wall in the living room with a complex set of wooden timbers. It was a major ptoject, considering she wanted us to build it ourselves. She began with a foundation of fiber matting on the wall. Then we had the timbers cut to her specifications. Each had to be stained and dried before mounting them on the walls.

But that wasn't enough for Sue. After living there a few years, she decided we had to move. She was antsy since this was the first house we occupied for more than one year. She actually wanted to buy the vacant lot across the street and build a new home on it, then move in. Fortunately, a cooler head (mine) prevailed.

We bought our house in Costa Mesa in 1975. By this time her art career was flourishing. So, she decided that the downstairs bedroom would become her studio. But it had to become much bigger to accommodate the etching press she envisioned needing. She had some walls knocked out, two outside doors installed, and added on 200 square feet to accommodate her planned storage bins, two giant work tables, an auxillary box to house the resin powder blown on the plate, a desk, and of course the humongous etching press. She required a large double sink and a heavy-duty fan to force the fumes from the acid to escape. Sue hired a contractor for the work, but supervised them daily.

She dicided we needed more light. So she had skylights instaled in the living room, the dining room, the kitchen, and both upstairs bathrooms. She completely modernized the kitchen, removing hanging cabinets betwwen the kitchen and breakfast area, white washing all reamining cabinets, and installing rollers under all drawers and pantry shelves. She replaced the flooring with title.

Sue replaced the livingroom window with a large beveled bay window. She replaced the front doors and foyer chandlelier and installed a curved decorative window above the doors. She also installed another curved decorative window over the kitchen door. She replaced the chandelier in the dining room and created a faux wall. She replaced the living room fireplace and mantel with a more modern structure. She also modified the fireplace in the family room. After removing the asbestos popccorn ceiling in the family room, she installed an artistic tile floor.

Years later, Sue hired a friend to install baseboard molding and crown molding throughout the house. She removed the wainscott in the master bedroom and raised the ceiling eight inches.Then she decided we needed a bigger master bathroom. She had a contractor knock out a bedroom wall to create a walk-in shower so big we could host a party in it. She replaced the fixtures in all three bathrooms and modernize them.

Then she really got going. She designed an enlarged family room, adding on another 200 square feet, and introduced nine more skylights She handed her sketches off to an architect, then used the plans to get bids from six contractors. We now had a 3200 square foot house for two people since the kids had left the nest.

Showing Off Her New Family Room to the Girls: Rachel, Karissa, Pam, Sue, Taylor, Sheryl

Sue put just as much thought in changing the outside of the house. She created a front brick walk and lined the the front yard with bricks to highlight her flower gardens. Then she designed hardscape for the entire backyard. We replaced several trees in the back yard with self pruning palm trees that ultimately grew to 30 feet. We installed a large gunnite jacuzzi embedded in the backyard, then later tiled it thoughout. We removed two large eucaliptus trees from the front yard to avoid them falling on the neighbors' house.

Why did I agree to all these changes? She paid for all of it with her art sales. Sue said if we didn't do them, we would have to move. She knew how to play me.

Moving to Reatta Glen in 2019 did not modify her adventurous addiction to change. Even though we did not really own our home, Sue still wanted to redo things. She first replaced the chandalier in the dining room.

Then she installed a ceiling light in the center of all three bedrooms -- one would be her studio; another, my office. For an extra lighting bonus, she replace all three hanging lights in the kitchen.

She soon bought outdoor furniture for the back patio, then expanded the concrete patio size to accommodate the new furniture. Then she decided that four closets were insufficient to hang all her clothes, so she hired California Closets to install a remote-controlled clothes bar to come down from the ten-foot-ceiling. She satisfied her desire for more change by redecorating the villa interior to coincide with each season of the year. Finally, she changed the deorations for the front patio every holiday. She stored these decorations in 23 plastic bages tacked to the walls of the garage.

Some of the Many Bags in Our Garage Housing Sue's Holiday Decorations

It may not be a surprise to learn that Sue's favorite channel became HGTV, the home design remodeling channel.

10. The World Traveler

When Sheryl left home for Cal Poly San Luis Obispo, Sue and I experienced our first taste of empty nesters. In 1986, we wasted no time in obtaining our first passports and began our international travel. I found Sue's wanderlust to be contagious. Ultimately, we visited 99 countries and enjoyed 44 cruises. Most of our trips were of two or three weeks duration. After one unpleasant international flight in coach class, we always traveled business class. We enjoyed many different cruise lines, but our favorites were Renaissance (no longer in business) and Regent

Seven Seas. Sue preferred the smaller ships over the huge ones.

Although all the cruises were fun with diverse ports of call, we agreed that we learned so much more from the land tours. They provided the most retentive memories of the countries. Overseas Adventure Travel became our guide of choice because we spent quality time with the local people and began to understand and appreciate their culture. With OAT we never had more than 14 fellow travelers with us, so we knew them well after two weeks. We traveled in a minibus which was spacious and convenient. Our guides were charismatic, knowledgeable, informative, and kept us safe. The accommodations were always pleasant and adequate, but not luxurious. Sue's relentless need for adventure was largely satisfied during the next 37 years.

Italy

Our first international trip was a three-week land tour of Italy with American Express. We were enthralled with the small medieval cities like Verona, Siena, and San Gimignano. Romantic Tuscany captured our hearts, and Florence did not disappoint; I even enjoyed the Uffizi Art Gallery, which was a real highlight for Sue. Seeing the Leaning Tower of Pisa impressed us both when I remembered that it was here that Galileo dropped two balls of significantly different mass to prove that gravity caused them to descend at the same rate, independent of weight.

The Pompeii site inspired Sue. Much of it seemed perfectly preserved when buried by the ash from Mt. Vesuvius' eruptions in 79 CE. Multicolored murals on so many walls were uncovered. The amount of pornography and the phallic symbols carved into the pathway to the brothel surprised me.

We have fond memories of the Vatican's Sistine Chapel, the Colosseum, the Trevi Fountain, the Spanish Steps, the Catacombs, and the Forum of Rome. The sixteenth century gardens and estate, Villa d' Este, in Tivoli impressed Sue. The owner had rerouted a river through the property to create innumerable fountains everywhere on his land.

Tivoli Gardens Fountains Everywhere with Sue, Mike, Merle, Kurth

In the Italian Alps we viewed arguably the three most beautiful lakes in the world: Lake Lugano, Lake Como, and Lake Maggiore. Of course, we also toured Milan. There we saw, just two feet in front of us, the **original** Leonardo da Vinci mural of *The Last Supper* on the end wall of the dining hall at the Monastery of Santa Maria delle Grazie. We could hardly believe it. Today they no longer let anyone near the painting.

China

Shortly thereafter, we booked a land tour of China, which was eye-opening. In Shanghai, Sue and I left the group to venture into a park next to our hotel. We were the only Americans, surrounded by Chinese, practicing Tai Chi and just enjoying the park. China had just been opened to tourists, so it appeared many were not accustomed to foreigners in their little park. Sue drew a crowd around her. They were fascinated by her blond hair. Two professors tried out their newly learned English on us. One of them sold us some local postcards.

In Beijing, we were impressed by the vast Tiananmen Square with the large poster of Mao Tse-tung prominently and centrally displayed at one end. We explored the forbidden city. Sue loved the little two- and three-year-old boys dressed like royalty with their cute little red caps. We were thrilled to walk on the Great Wall of China.

We sailed a Chinese junk boat down the Li River in Guilin. More than one hundred limestone "thumbs," up to 200 feet high, rising through the mist on the river made this surrealistic. This scene inspired Sue's artwork.

The Guilin River Backdrop

We flew to Xian to see the famous Terracotta Warriors. Although at that time there were less than 1,000 figures uncovered, the scene was impressive. Today another 1,000 have been found, but it is believed that another 6,000 are still buried. They were created 2200 years ago to defend China's first emperor in the afterlife and were buried in four pits less than one mile from the emperor's tomb. Although the warriors' bodies were cast from a few standard molds (standing, kneeling, driving a horse-drawn chariot), all their faces were unique and carved by hand. But there was so much pollution in Xian that almost all the residents wore facemasks.

We learned from the Italy and China trips how to improve our international travel experience. The American Express tour endured a full busload of 40 people. This detracted from our walking tours as well as the lengthy time disembarking, waiting for stragglers, and re-boarding. This inspired us to hire Overseas Adventure Travel in the future, with a maximum of 16 people. We did take one special Tauck tour, which was more upscale, but had 24 people in the group. Other wonderful luxury tours were conducted by Abercrombie and Kent.

Traveling on Our Own

The first time we tried international travel on our own was rather adventurous. I had accumulated several hundred thousand business miles on United Airlines by flying from California to my offices in Houston and Seattle and to our corporate headquarters in Boston. Now it was time to use these miles effectively. We flew first class on our first five trips to Asia and Europe using these free miles. First, we decided to explore two exotic cities in Asia which sounded adventurous and perfect for Sue: Singapore and Hong Kong on a single trip. And indeed, they were.

Singapore and Hong Kong

It took more than 18 hours to get to Singapore, but first class made it enjoyable: luxurious seats, great service, top-shelf cocktails, chilled vodka, excellent food, and pampering. Sue smiled for the whole trip. We spent five days in Singapore with a multiday bus pass, visiting the zoo and museums, shopping on Orchard Street, having a Singapore Sling at Raffle's, and exploring Sentosa Island via a cable car from the World Trade Center. Two unusual things struck us: the absolute cleanliness of all the streets and the sparsity of people. We learned we would be fined $500 for spitting out gum anywhere.

We spent a day at the Singapore wildlife reserve. Adventurous Sue let a man place a large black and green snake around her neck. I stayed clear.

She knows no fear.

Remarkably, this island city was reclaiming land from the ocean, building new upscale hotels (Our new Westin was only 1/3 full.), beginning to build their mass rapid transit system, and enhancing their infrastructure. These major investments paid off, as Singapore would soon become a magnet for adventurous world travelers. We have returned three more times in our travels and watched the city blossom, catering to tourists.

Hong Kong, the Pearl of the Orient, lived up to its nickname. We visited prior to Great Britain returning control of Hong Kong to China in 1997. Its vibrant economy, great shopping bargains, interesting people, and beautiful, exciting harbor viewed from Victoria Peak made this one of my favorite cities in the world. We stayed in the Hyatt on the Kowloon side of the harbor.

We took the 50-minute Russian hydrofoil to Macau for a few hours. At that time, it was a favorite place to gamble for the Chinese in Hong Kong. The housewives would go there for the day while their husbands were at work. It had only two casinos when we visited. Today with 36 casinos, it is the gambling capital of the world, surpassing Las Vegas.

Back in Hong Kong, we shopped 'til we dropped, buying jewelry, tailored new suits, and $20 4-ply cashmere sweaters for everyone we knew. Sue was in her element, shopping with glee! The tailor sent a bottle of Chivas Regal to our hotel as a thank you. We bought another large suitcase to haul it all home. Since that trip, we returned to Hong Kong three more times, but it has changed since becoming part of China in 1997. The people did not seem as energetic, and the prices were much higher.

France, Germany, and Switzerland

The first time we traveled to France, Germany, and Switzerland, we also ventured out on our own. We first spent four days exploring Paris, rented a car to discover Bavaria's Black Forest and the Swiss and French Alps, then down to Monaco and the French Riviera.

Paris was magical. We stayed in a two-story walkup, halfway between the Arc de Triomphe and the Eiffel Tower. We could see both from our room. We explored Paris, riding their excellent metro lines as well as on foot. Most impressive were the Seine, the Notre-Dame Cathedral, the Louvre (Sue's favorite, of course), the Eiffel Tower, Concord Square, the curbside cafes and expresso bars, the quaint shops and bookstores along the Right Bank of the Seine, and the narrow historic streets. Sue could have explored the Louvre forever -- me, not so much.

As a special treat, we decided to splurge and dine at a Michelin two star restaurant. We dressed up as best we could with our traveling clothes, hopped on to the Paris

Metro and got off on the Champs Elysees, noticing the Bentleys dropping impeccably dressed people, some in military dress uniforms, at our restaurant. We calmly walked in like we belonged there and were seated by our tuxedo-clad waiter. With our Berlitz book, we tried to decipher the menu. Sue recognized "canard" and ordered the duck with a salad and green beans. The waiter vehemently objected, pointing out that the green beans did not properly go with her entrée choice. Although we were not wine drinkers, we ordered the bottle of wine he suggested. After going through the first course, drinking several glasses of wine, we were feeling no pain when the entrees arrived. Sue's duck looked strange: two large slabs of exceptionally smooth meat. She liked it, not tasting like duck, but familiar. It was duck liver! The waiter pointed out the live large ducks in cages. Well, we finished the wine with our entrees and ordered another half bottle to go with our Grand Marnier souffle. Fortunately, we were taking the Metro home, or we might not have made it.

We spent an unforgettable day touring Versailles. The palace itself was breathtaking with its hall of mirrors, gold, crystal, and precious gem adornments, the Royal Chapel, and the amazing artwork. The vast gardens of Versailles impressed Sue with the rare flowers, sculptures, and fountains.

The next day we rented our car, a stick-shift Renault, and left Paris for the German Black Forest. After driving through beautiful Freiberg, we approached the little town of Triberg. We were forced to park our car outside the town. They were having their own little Octoberfest, and no traffic was allowed. We followed the residents to their party and joined in, although we could not speak a word of German. Picnic tables were laid out in front of the food booths. We made our selections, including the traditional Black Forest cake, and sat down with the Germans. I pointed to a man's stein of beer and animatedly asked where I could buy the beer. He got up and took me by the hand to the beer booth. An old-fashioned organ grinder was entertaining us with his pet monkey. This was a memorable stop on our journey through the Black Forest. Sue loved the setting – the German food, not so much.

We drove our little French car through the majestic Swiss Alps. We toured the Swiss heritage sites in Interlaken and spent the night on the shore of Lake Lucerne, viewing the historic bridges on the Reuss River.

Sue longed to replace the German food with French cooking, so we headed back into France at Lyon. We took full advantage of our Michelin Guide to find great French restaurants, denoted by the red *R* next to the name of the hotel. There we spent the night, usually in a spartan three-story walk-up, hauling our luggage. But the hotel was usually owned by a renowned chef, retired from Paris, whose meals were exquisite. I remember paying $80 for dinner and $20 for the room. Both were priced right. In the morning, Sue would shop at the little stores for bread, cheese, salami, and bakery. Then, with our newly acquired taste, we would buy a bottle of red wine for our lunch, all of which we consumed off the road as a personal picnic. Sue appreciated how friendly the merchants in these towns were, helping us struggle with our French and congratulating us when we got it right. So different from the rude Parisians.

When we finally made it down to the Mediterranean, we toured up and down the Riviera, noting the difference in their beaches. Our hotel room in Nice overlooked these beaches which. instead of sand, were smooth stones and pebbles. At lunch time we witnessed French women in business suits stripping off all their clothes to don bikini bottoms in preparation for their hour in the sun.

Of course, we drove up to beautiful Monaco and gambled at Monte Carlo, where I won five francs playing blackjack. But then, I absentmindedly drove down a street for pedestrians only. So, Sue took over the driving as we made our way up the mountainside overlooking Monaco. We wanted to get off this treacherous, narrow, two-lane mountain road to get back to Nice before sunset, but there were no turnoffs. We were relieved to see a sign that indicated to stay on the same road to reach the highway. So, Sue struggled with the Renault's stick shift on the three scenic corniches before reaching the top of the mountain. (Never again did we rent a stick shift.) She was sorry that she volunteered to drive.

On our last day in Nice, we became spectators for an Ironman Triathlon on the beach in front of our hotel. Here the start of the 2.4-mile ocean swim began. After the swim, the male contestants entertained Sue by stripping off their swimsuits to get into their racing togs for the 112-mile bicycle leg which finished at the starting place before beginning the 26.2-mile marathon run. We could not watch the finish, as we had to catch our flight back to the US.

Australia

We booked our own trip to Australia, a 14-hour flight to Sydney, connecting to Cairns in Queensland. We began with a tour of the Daintree rainforest in a DUKW or "duck," a six-wheeled amphibious 2½ ton WWII truck. This adventure fascinated Sue, spotting the unique species of flora and fauna in the dense, overcrowded rainforest floor.

Then we boarded a 69-passenger ship, the Coral Princess, for a four-day cruise on the amazing Great Barrier Reef and its islands. We had to delay our Australian trip one week because the ship was in dry dock waiting for a new propeller. We had only 36 passengers on board and a 25-year-old captain, the youngest in Australia. We were the only Americans. The other passengers were mostly Brits, Kiwis, and a few Germans. This trip both exhilarated and exhausted us, snorkeling on the reef every day, eating fresh seafood, including spiny lobsters, and fresh fruit.

I was up on the bridge with the captain when we navigated our last leg into Townsville, our final destination. He had the throttle wide open for the last few kilometers, as I noticed the tide going out and the sonar showing three, then two, then one, then ½ meter clearance! I surmised that this was why the last captain was fired; he ran aground and bent the propeller.

At Townsville we caught a flight to Brisbane on Australia's Gold Coast, connecting to Sydney. There we stayed at the Hyatt in Kings Cross in the Red-Light District, conveniently located to the Sydney Metro rapid transit system. The underground Metro was delightful, with musicians entertaining at some stops, including ours at the Kings Cross Station. We took the Metro to the Sydney Opera House for a concert, to the half-price ticket booths, and to the musical plays, which we thoroughly enjoyed. We also took day trips out of Sydney to the Blue Mountains and the outback. Most of all we enjoyed meeting real Aussies, quite friendly and interested in Americans. A national pastime is consuming their lager beer, principally Fosters, which Sue learned to chug down like a local. She called on her expert college training.

Before we left Australia, Sue HAD to hold a koala bear. She was warned these cute little guys can be vicious. But the only caution this adventurous lady took was to wear protective glasses.

The Koala Kid

New Zealand

Seven months later, we embarked on another self-reliant adventure to delightful New Zealand. We had heard how great the Kiwi people were, so we decided to try the bed and breakfast route. Based on travel agent bookings, the price of these accommodations seemed high. But the wise bird on Sue's shoulder advised us to wait until we arrived and book directly with the locals. So, we took a chance by advance booking only the first few days with the Hyatt chain, with which we had a frequent traveler discount, and leaving the rest of our itinerary open.

Once again, we flew the 14-hour, first class flight to Auckland, stayed at the Hyatt, and rented a car (with an automatic transmission). It would be hard enough to negotiate the wrong side of the road without the trauma of manipulating a stick shift. Sue agreed to share the driving. The first thing we did was to find the right bookshop to buy the guide to bed and breakfast places throughout the country. (Airbnb did not surface until twenty years later.) The wise bird was right again; the prices were a small fraction of what the agent quoted in the US. And the book described each domicile and its host in quaint detail, down to the description and name of its pets. We also purchased an NZ telephone card to enable booking the rest of our reservations.

The next day we drove to Rotorua, where we learned about the fascinating Māori. The Māori are the indigenous people who arrived from Polynesia during the 14th century. They are dark skinned with colorful clothing and elaborate skin decorations and tattoos. Although they brought their own culture of mythology, crafts, and performing arts, the Europeans arriving 400-600 years later influenced their culture, enabling a degree of coexistence. We found them quite friendly, and Sue admired their craftsmanship skills, especially in building canoes.

Colorful, Strange Māori

A direct descendent of a Māori chief guided us through the famous Waitomo glowworm cave on the central part of the North Island, 87 miles from Rotorua. The glowworms are unique in the world. We relaxed and laid back in a boat, floating through the cave's stream and looking up at the thousands of these creatures hanging from the cave's ceilings and lighting our way.

Sue loved the adventure of the caves and their glow worms.

We drove to Wellington, New Zealand's capital, at the southern tip of the North Island. En route we experienced first-hand the fact that there were seven times more sheep than people. Several times we had to stop the car to let a flock of sheep cross the road.

The owner checked us in to her B&B, then offered to take us on a tour of the town, of which she was immensely proud. We began to appreciate the friendliness and hospitality of these wonderful people.

The next morning, we dropped off our rental car to board the Cook Strait Ferry to take us to the South Island. This strait is considered one of the most dangerous and unpredictable waters in the world, although it is only 14 miles wide. It connects the Tasmanian Sea with the South Pacific Ocean. Our ferry only spent half the time in the strait; the rest of the three-hour, 43-mile journey was in the Marlboro Sounds, docking at Picton. Sue was a Mariner Scout and never got seasick, so I followed her lead. We were lucky to cross in good weather and made friends with two young Kiwi sailors onboard. We picked up our next rental car and gave our new friends a lift to Christ Church.

Christ Church is in the Canterbury Region on the South Island's east coast. Although it is New Zealand's second largest city, it seemed like a delightful, quaint small town, designed around the central Cathedral Square. Sue declared it her favorite. It became a city in 1856, laid out in a grid pattern around the square. We were saddened when it later suffered a series of major earthquakes during 2010-2012, demolishing 1,500 buildings and killing 185. It is still being rebuilt today. While staying in Christ Church, adventurous Sue decided we should take a helicopter ride around the spectacular glaciers of Mount Cook. It was expensive but so worth it.

The next day we motored south to the little town of Dunedin. We stopped to see the Royal Albatross Centre on the Otago Peninsula. I realized that Sue was becoming quite a "birder." This is the world's only mainland breeding colony for these special birds, who spend 85% of their lives at sea. We were able to approach them, astonished as to their size, weighing 22 pounds with a wingspan of up to 11 feet. We were in awe, watching them take off and land on the treacherous cliffs. They soared much like a glider. They are so big that they need the high winds on these cliffs to get airborne.

That evening we paid $3 to enter a farmer's land to view the penguins coming in from the sea to their nests. Rain was pouring down, and they were so far from our cliff viewpoint that they were hard to see. Sue didn't care; she absolutely loved the penguins.

The next day, driving farther south and inland, we reached exiting Queenstown. As we approached, we stopped to view people bungee jumping off the Kawarau bridge, where the sport originated in 1979. The brave jumpers are tied to the rope by their ankles and weighed to determine how much slack is required to stop their head just above the river's surface, some 142 feet down. One of the staff told us they used to allow the females to jump free of charge if they jumped in the nude. But they stopped offering the freebies when they had so many girls jumping that they lost money. I had to talk Sue out of trying this.

Although we declined on the first of a triad of events called the Super Triple Challenge (bungee jumping, sky diving and hang gliding), we did participate in the less outrageous standard triple challenge: the Shotover River jet boat ride, the helicopter through Skipper's Canyon, and the whitewater river rafting at Deep Creek.

Readying for the Shotover River Boat Rode

Sue 's adventurous spirit was somewhat satiated. As we neared the final stretch of rafting, the river became a Class V, and we had to hold on for dear life. They took our picture from the shore to capture the fear on our faces, but we were going backward and flying at the time.

NZ Whitewater

In our wetsuits, life jackets, and helmets, we resembled the "Teenage Ninja Turtles."

New Zealand Ninja Turtles

We stayed three nights in this fun, adventurous town, feeling old compared to the twentysomethings that dominated. We did take a more sedate boat trip through beautiful Milford Sound and its amazing waterfall before flying to Auckland for the trip home.

Spain

Spain was much more than we anticipated. We spent the first few days in Madrid exploring one of Sue's art museum treasures, the Prado. Then, we rented a car to drive a loop around southern Spain, ending back in Madrid. But we were warned to examine the tires of the rental before we started driving. Thieves posing as good Samaritans will make cuts in a tire, and when we stop to change the flat, they will offer to help as they rob us.

We stayed in paradors, luxury hotels that the government renovated at historical monasteries and castles or in locations with exceptional topography and view. We drove to Toledo, a UNESCO World Heritage Site, and the medieval "Imperial City" that was the capital of the province from 542 to 725 CE. Our parador overlooked the city. Throughout Toledo are markings showing the route of mythical Don Quixote.

Next, we drove down to Granada to see the Alhambra. The small parador here had no vacancy, so we had to drive 38 miles up a winding mountain road to stay in a parador at the Sierra Nevada Ski Station. The Alhambra is an Arab citadel and palace. It is the most famous building in Moorish Islamic history.

We then drove down to the Costa del Sol in Andalusia. We stopped in Malaga to shop, but when the proprietor learned we were driving a rental car, he told us to immediately get back to our car or the trunk would be forced open, and our luggage would be stolen.

We crossed over a bridge to the British Territory of Gibraltar, where we bought the Lladro Flower Cart piece that Sue had admired for years. It cost $2,500 at home, but only $1,000 in Gibraltar due in part to the omission of value-added tax. The problem now was to get the extremely fragile favorite of Sue's home in one piece without breaking the delicate porcelain flowers. As we drove up the Gibraltar grade, the car was inundated by Barbary

Rock Apes, the only wild primates in Europe. We were happy to get back to town safely.

We drove along the coast looking up at the high cliffs to see the beautiful white cities of Andalusia until we reached Cadiz and Valencia. We loved the environs of Valencia, but kept our windows closed and dared not stop, as we were told of thieves that zip by on mopeds to snatch purses or anything loose off our bodies as they race by. We did spend one night in Faro on the southern coast of Portugal, but it was unremarkable compared to the grandeur of Spain.

We stopped at Merida, the Spanish Roman capital in 25 CE. We were surprised by the excellent condition of the Roman ruins, second only to Rome. Notable were the Puente Romano, the oldest existing Roman bridge, the Forum, the Temple of Diana, the Circus Maximus, the Amphitheater, and the National Museum of Roman Art, containing wonderful Roman artifacts.

We drove north to discover the city of Avila, 3700 feet above sea level, a Sue favorite. It is surrounded by medieval walls where several movies were filmed. It is another UNESCO World Heritage Site.

We drove only 40 miles east to explore the small city of Segovia. It sports a magnificent fairy castle, the Alcazar of Segovia, which looked quite familiar; it was a template for Disney's Cinderella Castle. Sue thought she was in a movie. Another great landmark is the 2500-foot-long first century Roman aqueduct with 170 arches, another UNESCO World Heritage Site.

When we returned to Madrid, Air Force One held up our flight, as George Bush landed to visit the prime minister of Spain.

All Inclusive Resorts

Acapulco

After visiting a Club Med for dinner in Kauai, we decided to try one in Mexico, just North of Acapulco. Spartan accommodations and unremarkable cuisine enabled low cost, but it was pure fun. We were in our thirties, still young enough to mingle with the younger couples and staff, called GOs. We played tennis, learned how to sail in a one-man Sunflower, snorkeled, and bought drinks with plastic beads around our necks, so we did not need cash-ladened pockets in our swimsuits.

Standard Club Med Attire

While enjoying the beautiful sunsets, we would get an umbrella drink, sit back in our hammocks, and watch Sue's favorite pelicans fly in time to the classical music from the speakers. It was magical. Every night we would all gather before dinner to sing and dance to their zany songs, like the chicken dance and *YMCA*. But mid-week the Mexican Fedcrales confiscated our windsurfing boards because Club Med would not pay the $100 per board ransom to get them returned. They confiscated all the tennis balls the previous week for the same reason. But we had so much fun, we decided to do another.

On our way home our plane was late, missing our connection in Mexico City. So, we had to spend the night. Mexicana Airlines would not reimburse us, so someone from the Holiday Inn offered to give us a package deal for $200 per person. I asked the airline attendant if we could get something cheaper. We took a $2 cab ride to a hotel in a poor part of town. After we checked in and I saw the prices on the menu, I told Sue to dress up for dinner. We were greeted by tuxedo-clad waiters, ordered cocktails, chateaubriand for two, and a great dessert. We had an excellent meal, drinks, and a nice room for a total of $35 for the two of us! Lesson learned: do not accept an unsolicited accommodation deal at an airport just because it is convenient.

Playa Blanca

A few years later Sue convinced our friends, Don and Vanda Peterson, to join us at the Club Med in Playa Blanca, Mexico. It was equally enjoyable. We started with a bus ride from the Mazatlán airport. The Club Med bus stopped in town to enable us to "stock up" with Tequila and beer for the two-hour trek over a narrow, dangerous dirt road. Upon arrival Vanda instantly loved it. We immediately got into our swim gear and almost never wore anything else the whole week.

Playa Blanca Beauty

Playa Blanca was just as spartan with twin beds and straw mattresses. This time Sue and I knew all the songs and dances, which added to our enjoyment. This club was primarily populated by couples, often unmarried, as we learned by their clothes optional solarium and beach. The rooms were only locked from the inside. We heard the girl next door trying to get her roommate and boyfriend to open the door so she could retrieve her clothes for the night. One night we learned about tequila "slammers" which we all imbibed before playing volleyball by spotlight.

Along the beach we rode horses who set their own pace: slowly on the way out and extremely fast on the way back. We had fun going deep sea fishing, but of course Sue caught all the fish. We decided another Club Med would be in our future.

Paradise Island

Once again, Don and Vanda joined us for a Club Med on Paradise Island across from Nassau in the Bahamas. This was a little more upscale, but still inexpensive. One thing we did was quite different here. We took an excursion off campus, where we each donned an old-fashioned diving helmet connected to a land-based air tube. We went 15 feet under water, walked along the bottom of the sea, and stood still with our arms extended as a giant grouper swam into our arms and posed for the picture.

Sue Calmly Holding the Vicious Grouper

Club Med was located adjacent to the new Atlantis Resort. So, we were able to play some blackjack before we flew home.

Puerto Rico

We joined Sue's parents at El Conquistador, a beautiful resort on the east end of Puerto Rico. The hotel is located on a 300-foot cliff overlooking the Caribbean, but one can take a fun funicular down the cliff to reach the beach and golf course. We loved it there, playing golf and beaching. But this was the place that Sue insisted on leaving for a day to win a lot of money at the San Juan Racetrack, using her special knowledge of horses.

We spent some time gambling at the Mayaguez Casino before returning to El Conquistador. The casino was unique with dark, cozy individual booths along the casino floor.

Dominican Republic

We joined Sue's sister, Sandy, and brother-in-law, John for a strange itinerary to get to the all-inclusive Excellence Resort in Punta Cana. We left balmy Southern California to fly to Winneconne, Wisconsin in February to join their group. So, we wore our winter coats to go to a tropical climate in the Caribbean. The group was fun, so it was worth it — maybe?

Not Wisconsin Winter Attire

The magnificent resort offered six restaurants, upscale liquor, and an enormous pool. We played a few silly, but fun games. Sue used the special talent she learned at the UW pub to win the chug-a-lug beer drinking contest.

Sue and I managed to capsize a catamaran sailboat and had to be rescued. We took a tour of the island to break the monotony. The week was relaxed and slow-moving. But we were not anxious to return to the Wisconsin winter.

Jamaica

We spent a more active week at the Breezes Resort in Ocho Rios with Sandy and John. We always enjoyed John and Sandy's company.

Sandy, John, Kurth, Sue

We were able to play 36 holes of golf. We got soaked negotiating the water trek up Dunn's River Falls, walking uphill against the river current. It was reminiscent of the first time we visited Breezes on our own, a beautiful, romantic place.

Guided Land Tours

Our trips with a professional guide were every bit as enjoyable as the land trips we did on our own. Most of these were with Overseas Adventure Travel, which guarantees a group with never more than 16 passengers. This feature, their excellent guides, and the promise of adventure always made these trips memorable. Visiting the local schools and homes gave an insight into their cultures that would not be possible in a large group. In addition, sharing the adventures with a small group enabled closer relationships with one's fellow travelers.

Thailand

Our first trip with OAT was two weeks in Thailand. Our guide was a young man, who had served two months in a monastery as a celibate, ordained Buddhist monk prior to his marriage, as was required in the Thai culture. Ninety percent of all Thai are Buddhists. This explains why we were shown so many wats (temples) and statues of Buddha in various positions, some of which were extraordinary: the emerald Buddha made entirely of jade, the 300-foot giant sitting Buddha, the 150-foot reclining Nirvana Buddha, and the solid gold Buddha. Ultimately, Sue had seen enough Buddhas and wats. She refused to get out of the vehicle to see another one.

Bangkok is one of the world's most fascinating cities with dazzling temples, a world-famous floating market, spectacular palaces, shrines, a colorful Chinatown, and much humidity. We rode several longtail boats (I called them the sore tail boats.) with outboard motors to get around the crowded city much more efficiently than any other type of transportation. We dined at interesting restaurants with scrumptious seafood, but we also dined with a Thai family in their home.

My three-hour massage recommended by our guide was not pleasant. An extravaganza of the Siam Niramit show dazzled us the final night before we motored north to explore the famous bridge over the River Kwai and the Death Railway. Unfortunately, we viewed the corresponding museum of the macabre conditions imposed by the Japanese on the allied WWII POWs.

Then we continued north to the majestic mountainous Golden Triangle near Chiang Rei on the border of Laos and Burma (now Myanmar). This used to be the location of the largest poppy region for opioids and heroin in the world.

We then traveled to Chiang Mei for a fabulous one-hour ride on an elephant. Like the other travelers in our group, we bought a bunch of bananas to feed the elephant. He knew Sue had them, so he continued searching through her jacket with his trunk. If he found the bunch, he would devour it whole, but by feeding him one-at-a-time, he would peel each with his dexterous trunk before stuffing it into his mouth. We thoroughly enjoyed the ride on this gentle giant through the jungle and across a river.

Our Elephant Searching for Sue's Bananas

We dismounted to an elephant camp where they put on a show for us. The next day we flew back to Bangkok for the long flight home.

Costa Rica

OAT surprised us with a real adventure in Costa Rica. Costa Rica is easily the most developed of the Central American countries. I was surprised to learn its major industries include manufacturing of integrated circuits.

Our guide was an amateur astronomer, who loved to show us the night sky. He took us through the Costa Rica mountains and jungles, pointing out the unique birds, plants, and trees. The long line of giant black ants crossing our path, each with a leaf segment bigger than its body on its back, was particularly impressive. Our guide explained that they were taking food to their nest, would chew and store it, then eat it during the winter.

The 16 of us boarded a small open-air boat and were introduced to a river guide. We encountered many beautiful native butterflies along the river, including the famous Blue Morpho, one of the largest and most recognizable in the world. There were several crocodiles in the river. When we approached a 15-foot crock which the guide seemed to recognize, he turned the boat and headed to the bank. He disembarked and started slapping the water with the dressed half chicken which he brought along, while backing up toward the bank. The swimming crock made a right-angle turn, heading for the guide double time. The guide continued to back up while the crocodile fixated on him and the chicken, When the crock reached the shore, he opened his gigantic mouth just inches from the guide. Then, he let go of the chicken. The crocodile slammed his jaws shut with the chicken inside and took off down the river. I asked the guide about the large scar on his leg. He explained that once there were two crocodiles!

Our guide took us in his 20-passenger van to the base of a semi-active volcano, called Poas, which has erupted dozens of times since 1828. After driving to the base, we climbed up the last part of the rim to almost 7,000 feet to peer over the edge of the cauldron in which a pool of emerald-green water collected in the center. Steam escaped around the sides of the pool, a frightening sight.

Our next adventure experienced rafting in one of the best whitewater rivers in the world. Sue was excited, but I was nervous. We donned our life jackets and received our paddles as we took on two more guides in our two inflatable rafts. At first the river was reasonably calm, enabling us to enjoy the lush vegetation as we paddled through the rainforest. Midway, we stopped for lunch. The two guides went into the forest and came out with two small colorful frogs in their hands. While they appeared cute and attractive, the guides explained they were deadly. Natives would just touch the frogs' backs with their darts and use blow guns to kill their enemies on contact. Yes, they did wash their hands before serving us lunch. Back into the rafts for a rougher ride down the river, but still fun.

Whitewater Terror: Sue and Mike Upfront, Merle and Kurth Behind

We drove to our hotel near Costa Rica's most active volcano, Arenal. It is striking, rising 5,437 feet above the surrounding flatland. It erupts almost daily, and for us it did not disappoint. That evening we witnessed a spectacular eruption, setting the night sky aglow.

Sue and our friend, Mike, decided to join the more adventurous group to trek up 1,000 feet to board a zipline through the forest. Mike's wife, Merle, and I decided to take a safer option and have a massage. Sue loved it. She ziplined down through 11 stations, coming nose-to-nose with howler monkeys in the trees. Our massage was not as much fun as we got manhandled by a blind masseuse.

Sue can't stop smiling, getting ready for our ride with a stretching exercise.

Cowgirl Sue and her entourage mounted horses and rode to the mud baths. We drank beer while mud bathing in the warm springs, then showered to get the mud off. At the end of the day, we rode the horses back to our camp, observing tree sloths along the way.

She is in her element, leading us all to the mud bath via horseback.

The final full day ended with our guide and driver taking us to a pinnacle in the Palo Verde National Park overlooking the Pacific Ocean for a spectacular view. There we spotted a pair of the rare and endangered scarlet macaws. The plumage of these overgrown parrots is striking and can be easily seen from a distance. But there they were, perched in a tree less than 100 feet away. Sue, the birder, was fascinated. To top off the evening, our guide hooked up some opera music to a speaker in the van and passed out a local coffee liqueur called Britt. Perfect!

Then we had our farewell dinner. We were all jazzed up for a good time. Sue and I take two small, portable three-legged chairs with us wherever we go. This enables us to sit directly in front of the guide to listen to his narrative without blocking the view of our fellow travelers. But this guide did not like it. None of us could figure out why. So, while we were all drinking and having a great time, we commanded the guide and driver to sit in our two chairs as if they were in the van, while we roasted them unmercifully. Everyone thoroughly enjoyed this event except the guide.

Ireland

We teamed up with Mike and Merle and another couple, Al and Luray, to take an OAT trip through Ireland. We spent the entire two weeks touring the scenic southwest part of the island, mostly in County Cork and County Kerry. Our female guide loved her country as did we by the time we completed the tour. Our driver introduced us to Guinness, which eventually I liked; Sue -- not so much. We ended up buying the driver a pint wherever we went.

Of course we visited the 600-year-old Blarney Castle. Adventurous Sue was the first to hang upside down to kiss the Blarney Stone. I refused to kiss it when they told me that 1,000 people do it every day. (Today, it is disinfected each day.) Plus, it was a little scary for someone with a fear of heights since you had to be held upside down three stories up to do so. It was enough for me to negotiate the narrow spiral staircase to get up there.

We visited the Jameson distillery in Middleton, County Cork, where Merle and I volunteered to try six different kinds

Blarney Castle Adventure

of whiskey. Then Merle convinced them to add a seventh: their expensive blend of Irish whiskey. We two were feeling no pain the rest of the day. Sue didn't like the taste.

We toured the bustling town of Killarney and stopped at a pub for a pint of Guinness, carefully poured to ensure the foam is settled and skimmed off to fill the pint to the brim with pure Guinness. In Kearney National Park, we toured the impressive stately Muckross House. We explored several castles and learned why the Irish hated the English, reciting the destruction performed by Cornwallis and his troops in the 18th century.

Mike, Al, and I attempted to play golf at a local course. We rented clubs and gave it a valiant try in a howling, but typical, Irish wind. But the greens were the worst of it, elevated and hard as cement, not your typical California course. There was no way for your beautiful shot to hold. We finished 18 holes, but I refuse to reveal our scores. Sue wisely declined to join us.

We toured the city of Cobh in County Cork and learned that the Titanic left from this last port after departing from Southampton, England. Also, from here three million people emigrated from Ireland due to the potato famine in 1845-9.

We drove the 120-mile Ring of Kerry to enjoy the scenery of lakes, castle ruins, beaches, glens, mountains, and ocean. The incomparable beauty of the nearly vertical Cliffs of Moher is the highlight of County Clare. They are 700 feet above the Atlantic and run for five miles along the coast.

From there we drove through the town of Limerick, where we all invented our own limericks and recited them on the bus. Mine was not original, except I inserted the name of our female guide. "There once was a maid from Madras, who had a fine little ass. Not round and pink, as you might think, but had ears, a long tail, and ate grass." Merle created several original ones but, like many limericks, are not printable in mixed company.

At one hotel we were entertained when one of our party (Luray) got up in the middle of the night, looking in the dark for the loo (restroom), but locking herself in the closet instead. She made a lot of commotion before Al let her out. We recreated this story and the appropriate corresponding limericks on the flight home.

Israel and Jordon

This may have been my favorite OAT trip. However, Osama Bin Laden was killed as we were en route to Jordon. So, the guide told us to be careful with our short walk from our hotel to a local restaurant because there could be some terrorists who might not look kindly on a pair of Americans. Adventurous Sue was not intimidated. But we did notice the restaurant guard carrying an Uzi. When we got back to the hotel, we learned that only nine of our fellow travelers had signed up for the Jordon extension. This made the tour even better.

We spent our first full day exploring the well-preserved Roman ruins in Amman and Jerash. We did not realize that, before Christ, the Romans under Pompeii had conquered and transformed these towns into beautiful, stately, prosperous cities. Sue was especially impressed by Hadrian's Arch, the remains of the Hippodrome where they still hold chariot races with people dressed as gladiators and Roman centurions, the 3,000 seat south theater, and the Forum with 56 pillars. We also admired the Temple of Hercules inside the Amman Citadel with two complete 30-foot pillars.

Roman Ruins of Jerash

We had dinner in a Muslim home and learned some of their culture. The mother spoke little English, but her two daughters were proficient. Their father was divorced from their mother but lived upstairs with his new wife. The daughters, 27- and 29-years-old, were unmarried and living at home. Both were well-educated and professional. The younger daughter was engaged to be married. Her fiancé had to prove he could support her in their own home and had to give the family gold as an inverse dowry. Therefore, the Jordanian Muslims marry late in order to amass sufficient wealth as a prerequisite to marriage. We were surprised at their modern, western dress, no burkas nor significant coverings of their faces or bodies.

The highlight of Jordon and the main reason for adding it to our Israel tour was the UNESCO World Heritage Site of Petra. But first, we stopped in the north section of the Petra Archaeological Park to visit the site known as

Little Petra. Like Petra itself, but much smaller, it displays 2,000-year-old buildings carved into the walls of the 1,480-foot-long sandstone canyon. Excavated in the mid-20th century, the carvings have been amazingly well preserved, even with excellent detailed art in some rooms and frescos in the ceiling. The high walls through the narrow canyon emitted little sunlight. There we witnessed workers setting up for a Jordanian wedding that night.

As one of the New Seven Wonders of the World, Petra itself took our breath away. It remained unknown to the Western world until 1812. It is believed to have been established in 312 BCE. It was the capital of the nomad Nobataeans and a major regional trading hub with an estimated 20,000 inhabitants. It fell to the Romans in 106 CE. It is best known for its majestically preserved "Treasury" carved into the sandstone cliff. A massive theater is also remarkable. Several homes carved into the walls are prominent. Adventurous Sue happily rode a camel up the wadi back to the bus.

Crossing into Israel from Jordon was unexpected. The Israeli security displayed both friendliness and efficiency. They gave us the option of not stamping our passports. They explained that a passport stamped from Israel could give us problems if we wanted to enter a Muslim country, or even Palestinian territory. So, we elected to just stamp a separate document, so that the passport would not indicate that we had entered Israel. We were then transferred from the Jordanian guide to an Israeli guide, a thirty-something woman, who, like all young Israelis, had served two years in the Israeli military. She was cordial and friendly, but her military training was apparent.

We had stimulating face-to-face contact with such a diverse group of people in Israel that it seemed like we were not visiting such a tiny country, but many countries.

We had dinner with a young, ultra-orthodox Hasidic Jew with his black curly braids dangling down the sides of his face and dressed in his black hat and robe. He explained his sole purpose is to be a scholar of the Torah and Talmud, which he studied daily, while his wife supported him. (Sue was not impressed.) He aspired to follow all 613 commandments of the Torah (The Law).

We spent two hours with a Holocaust survivor, had lunch with a Bedouin family, met 1½ hours with an angry Palestinian, and had lunch with a Druze family just one day before their village was overrun by Lebanon terrorists. We spent two nights in a beautiful Kibbutz overlooking the Sea of Galilee. The first night we had dinner with the Kibbutz leader. He explained that when they first arrived from Russia, they were a communist Kibbutz, but quickly converted to socialism. Then, when they realized their best workers were leaving, they became a capitalist Kibbutz and greatly prospered ever since.

We went down the Golan Heights to board a boat to cross the biblical Sea of Galilee where Jesus performed his miracles. Fed by the Jordon River at the north, it is the lowest freshwater lake in the world, 700 feet below sea level and 33 miles in circumference. The Israeli captain was hospitable and played Christian hymns, including *How Great Thou Art,* on the boat's loudspeaker as we crossed. Sue was moved.

At the south end of the lake, Galilee flows back into the Jordon, which then flows south through the West Bank and into the Dead Sea at an elevation of 1,300 feet below sea level, the lowest elevation of water on earth. It is also one of the saltiest bodies of water on earth at 34%, almost ten times as salty as the ocean. There we floated effortlessly on our backs — what an amazing feeling. I had trouble convincing Sue that she had had enough. We also witnessed adult baptisms with total immersion upstream in the Jordon.

We were anxious to visit Jerusalem. We first walked the Via Dolorosa in the Old City, the nine Stations of the Cross inside the city believed to be the exact route Jesus took bearing his cross to his crucifixion. Sue was in awe. It was solemn but rushed. Our guide explained we had to stay ahead of Palestinian protestors who had gathered at Lion's Gate because a 17-year-old Palestinian terrorist had been killed by the Israeli Army the previous day. Next, we found the 1,600-foot-long, 62-foot-high Wailing Wall, a part of the original Western Wall, the only remains of the biblical Second Temple of Jerusalem created by Herod the Great in 19 BCE. The "Wailing Wall" is a western term to depict the Israelis mourning the destruction of their temple by the Romans in 70 CE. It is sacred to the Israelis who form lines (one for the men, another for women) to place their written prayers into crevices in the wall, as we both did.

We traveled five miles south of Jerusalem to Bethlehem for a day, which Sue greatly anticipated. But it was not as enthralling as I had hoped. Since Bethlehem was in Palestinian territory in the West Bank, we had to trade our Israeli guide for a Palestinian. We saw the Church of the Nativity, originally constructed in 339 CE to mark the place of Jesus' birth, as one of the holiest places in Christendom. The church has been a Christian pilgrimage from Jerusalem for 1,700 years. We walked down a hot, narrow passage under the church to an opening said to be the location of the manger of baby Jesus. Sue was thrilled. Then we went out to Shepherd Field a few miles from Bethlehem, believed to be the location where the angels announced Jesus' birth to the shepherds. But the actual location was speculation.

We traveled three miles south of Bethlehem to visit a striking ancient palace, the Herodian. Here, Herod the Great built his palace fortress between 23 and 15 BCE 2,500 feet above sea level. After exploring the top of the structure, we ventured down steep stairs into the gigantic cistern, built to house the water necessary to survive at the edge of the Judean desert. The size of this colossal creation amazed me.

We reentered Israel to visit Masada, the hilltop fortress under siege by the Roman Army in 73 CE. It was the location of one of the last conflicts between the Israelis and the Roman Empire. Thousands of Roman soldiers and their slaves eventually stormed the sect of Jewish Zealots in Masada to put down the Jewish rebellion. But the 960 Sicarii rebels killed themselves, rather than be captured and enslaved.

OAT held our farewell dinner in modern Tel Aviv overlooking the beautiful Mediterranean before the long flight home. I would recommend that Israel be on the short list of any world traveler whenever peace breaks out in the Middle East.

Prague and Bratislava

We toured Eastern Europe for the first time since the fall of the Soviet Union. Czechoslovakia had recently split into the Czech Republic and Slovakia. The beauty of Prague, the Czech Republic capital, impressed both of us. It is called the city of 100 spires. At night we would walk to the heart of the historic district, Old Town Square, to admire the Gothic churches, spires, and colorful baroque edifices. The medieval astronomical clock in the square center gave animated shows every hour. The Charles Bridge spans the Vltava River. Built in the ninth century, Prague Castle is particularly impressive. It is the largest castle in the world at 750,000 square feet, containing the Bohemian Crown Jewels. We were both disappointed when our young guide told us that the population has been steadily turning from Christianity since the early 20th century. It is now one of the least religious countries in Europe at 20% of the population, Christianity being less than 12%. We mistakenly surmised that after they got rid of the oppression of communism, they would be returning to a strong Christian majority.

Bratislava, the capital of Slovakia is only 45 miles from Vienna, Austria. Compared to glamorous Prague, it could be disappointing and mundane. But it turned out to be a fun city that we would not forget. On our way to the city, we made our own head gear out of balloons, under the tutelage of a member of our group who was a professional balloon artist. Sue's was quite creative, of course.

We had been invited to a mock wedding to experience their customs. After the ceremony at the church, we retrieved and donned our head gear and some bubble-blowing paraphernalia. We walked with the wedding party to the reception in a music hall, blowing bubbles along the way to the delight of the children who began following our procession. By the time we reached the reception, we were all jacked up. They loved our wild hats and invited us to dance with the wedding party — mostly polkas. We presented our balloon hats to the wedding guests and bubbles to the children. For us it was the highlight of Bratislava.

Peru and Galapagos

Our tour began at 11,000 feet in the Andes at Cuzco, Peru, the 13th century center of the Incan Empire. Sue and I had prepared for the altitude by spending a night before we left at 7,000 feet in Big Bear in the California mountains and also brought altitude sickness pills. But it was not enough. Soon after we arrived, we started feeling ill. Our guide gave us a drink made with cocoa beans and had us lie down for two hours. Although we were concerned about getting high on cocoa beans, it worked, and we felt great. Sometimes local cures trump prescribed medication. Later we watched a shaman, a native Peruvian spiritual leader, get high smoking cocoa to enable his "altered state of consciousness" to interact with the spiritual world.

The guide took us to a typical indigenous Peruvian Andes home: dirt floor with pet guinea pigs running around. (These pets eventually doubled as food for the native family.)

We climbed up to 12,000 feet altitude to the ruins of a citadel adjacent to and north of Cuzco called Saqsaywaman, a UNESCO World Heritage site. The Incas built it in the twelfth and thirteen centuries. It contains a giant plaza with three immense 20-foot-high terrace walls built from huge stones remaining after decimation of the complex by the Spaniards. The 100- to 200-ton stones were carefully fit together without mortar, yet so tight I could not fit a single piece of paper between them, nor fit a pin in their joints. They have survived Peru's devastating earthquakes.

We visited the villages of the native Peruvian tribes in the Sacred Valley of the Incas at a 12,500-foot altitude to learn how the indigenous people traditionally weaved their bright-colored blankets, hats, and clothes. Sue loved the tribesmen displaying their colorfully adorned llamas and entertaining us with a one-man band. I now know where some of the lyrics to the song, "Come Fly With Me" originated. We saw some of the woven items offered to us when our train to "The Lost City of the Incas" made stops along the route. Sue bought some souvenir treasures.

Our train from Cuzco to Machu Picchu went down through the Andes in switchback fashion to compensate for the dramatic grade. Machu Picchu is less than 8,000-feet altitude and 50 miles northwest of Cuzco. We spent the night at the base of the mountain, then switchback-ascended in a bus to the UNESCO World Heritage Site the next morning.

This amazing ancient city on top of a mountain was constructed circa 1450 CE but abandoned by the Incas 100 years later when they were conquered by the Spaniards. It was rediscovered in 1911, when the overgrowth of the forest began to be cleared. Restoration continues today. It is now one of the New Seven Wonders of the World. The ruins of nearly 200 buildings on terraces on two distinct levels surround the central square. Most impressive are the Temple of the Sun and the Room of the Three Windows. Another mountainous landscape, Huayna Picchu, rises less than a mile from the complex to 8,800 feet.

The setting was particularly breathtaking for me, due to my acrophobia. Two other women in our group were also afraid of heights. I dubbed us the "Sure-Footed California Wall Huggers," as our hands received insect bites from hanging on to every vegetation-covered wall as we navigated the scary complex. Sue had no trouble with the height and laughed at our anxiety. Two insane adventurers of our group, a couple from England, actually climbed up the adjacent worn, narrow, fragile, stone staircase to the top of Huayna Picchu. But they received many insect bites on their legs for their trouble.

Sure-Footed California Wall Hugger

As we re-boarded our bus, we were challenged by two native boys that they could beat the bus down the mountain on foot. Indeed, they did by running straight down the treacherous slope, while the bus was negotiating a switchback route. Sue was happy to pay them for their ambitious challenge and our entertainment.

Then we were off to Quito, Ecuador for a flight to the Galapagos Islands, 600 miles due west on the equator. Since our group consisted of only 14 people, we were joined on the Galapagos boat by the Spanish ambassador to Equator and his attractive young wife. She became a handful for our poor guide. He instructed us as to how important it was to stay quiet on the well-marked path to not disturb the vast diversity of wildlife. She ignored his admonitions.

Our new boat was cheaply made, and minor pieces kept falling off. The rough weather made the trips between the islands uncomfortable with furniture inside the second deck staterooms bouncing off the walls.

In 1835, Charles Darwin surveyed these islands in his boat, *HMS Beagle*. In 1859, he authored his famous book, *The Origin of the Species*. We spent seven days exploring eight of these amazing islands and their approachable and diverse wildlife. There were so many marine iguanas of every color that we had to be careful not to step on them. Because one was required to only walk on the defined paths (except the ambassador's wife who would flit everywhere except on the paths), the animals had no fear. Many cannot be found elsewhere. Most of the islands were uninhabited. We approached within three feet of an albatross chick in its nest. The bright red, orange, and yellow Grapsus crab was easy to spot on San Cristóbal Island. We swam with the playful Galapagos Sea Lions and sunned ourselves next to them on the beaches. The Galapagos islands are dry, mostly hardened lava. Therefore, Darwin's finch may sit on your shoulder to get any water you may have. The blue-footed booby is spectacular with his bright blue feet and mating dancing skills. But most dramatic is the 900-pound Galapagos giant tortoise, who lived more than 100 years. Sue was enthralled by these animals and the Brit in our group who posed none-to-nose with the largest one.

The chilly 69-degree water temperature did not deter us from swimming with the sea creatures off the boat. I did my best to restrain adventurous Sue. The ambassador's wife braved it in her tiny bikini. But three of our seventy-something female passengers entertained us with a water ballet that displayed real expertise in the sport. The sea lions seemed to enjoy it as well.

Japan

We spent two weeks exploring Japan, one of Sue's favorite OAT trips. Although the Japanese are very nationalistic, discouraging citizenship for non-Japanese, they were outwardly quite friendly. But their demographics have been hurting the country because their birth rate is low, and their population is aging. As a result, racism and xenophobia are on the decline and more foreign nationals are now being accepted as citizens.

We noticed that the Japanese were well-dressed and well-groomed, but many wore face masks in Tokyo, even though pollution did not appear to be a problem. We had lunch at the home of a gracious elderly couple. His trophies as a marathon runner adorned the room. Sue was impressed with their affable hospitality.

We spent two nights at a traditional Japanese guest house in the mountains of Hakone. We had to remove our shoes at the door, then don slippers and a yukata robe to enter. Furniture was sparse with a low table for dining on the floor. On the tatami-mat floor were traditional futons on which to sleep — a unique experience. Sue did not have a problem with this lifestyle.

We burned incense in the Shinto shrine on the shore of Lake Ashi. On the third morning, we boarded a cable car to climb up the mountainside. As we reached the apex, we received a spectacular view of iconic Mount Fuji as it penetrated the bank of clouds that usually hide this perfectly shaped volcano. We took a 200-mph bullet train, one of the fastest in the world, to Kanazawa. It was right on time and accelerated smoothly — very impressive.

Our final stop was the beautiful city of Kyoto. We timed this perfectly as it was the peak of cherry blossom time. The petals fell all around us as we walked through a sand and rock garden. It was enchanting. Sue could not have been more pleased. The next day as we headed for the Osaka airport, the rain brought virtually all the blossoms down.

Central America – the Mayans

Our guide greeted us at the San Salvador airport in El Salvador. His nickname was Rambo, which we learned to be appropriate. He was a mercenary. He had set up the jungle setting for the *Survivor* TV show.

Here, we visited our first Mayan dwelling, Joya de Cerein, which, like Pompeii, had been buried under 20 feet of volcanic ash for 1,500 years. The next day we drove to Honduras to explore the ancient city of Copan, another UNESCO World Heritage Site. It occupies 37 acres, initially built by a Mayan king in 426 CE and modified by successive kings for the next 400 years. At the central plaza is an acropolis surrounded

I'm not climbing it!

by temples. The Temple of the Hieroglyphic Stairway is a pyramid of 2,000 glyphs carved into 63 ascending steps. The city is known for the 166 stelae images (tall, sculptured monuments to prominent Mayans), mostly located along the processional way of the central plaza.

As we crossed the border into Guatemala, Rambo had to use his influence with his guns displayed, giving small bribes to the border guards. We cruised the deepest lake in Central America, Lake Atitlan, and enjoyed its beauty. Then we drove on to another UNESCO World Heritage Site, Antigua, to explore the La Merced ruins. After visiting Guatemala City, we traversed the rainforest to Tikal, another 1,800-year-old Mayan UNESCO World Heritage Site. It boasts of over 1,000 buildings (many not yet excavated) covering 23 square miles, including the giant ceremonial Lost World Pyramid and the 240-foot-high Temple of the Grand Jaguar. One female in our group was quite an athlete. She ran up the narrow stairs to the top, but none of us, not even adventurous Sue, dared to follow.

We traveled to the site of Cahul Pech in Belize as our last stop. It too has a central acropolis, surrounded by 34 structures. It was built as early as 1200 BCE. Its tallest temple is 80 feet. Excavation began in 1988. Belize is a fun place with restaurants along the beach on sand stilts and good snorkeling along the reefs, which appealed to Sue.

Kenya Safari

This was one of our best land tours, although it was not guided by OAT. Instead, Abercrombie and Kent were hired by the now defunct cruise line, Renaissance. They chartered a modified 737 for exactly 114 passengers (the capacity of their ship), which took us to Kenya, the Seychelles, and Egypt in 1997. Abercrombie and Kent did not disappoint.

I anticipated the highlight would be our small cruise ship sailing through the beautiful Seychelles in the Indian Ocean. Indeed, we did enjoy the Seychelles. We hired a fishing boat to take us out to the middle of the Indian Ocean where Sue caught the beautiful dorado (mahi mahi).

I thought the safari in Kenya would not be as exciting, likely having to look through field glasses trying to spot the distant animals while riding in a Range Rover; then having to spend several nights in a crummy tent. I could not have been more wrong.

In Nairobi, we had dinner at the Carnivore Restaurant where they served every type of game on a long skewer: hartebeest, crocodile, ostrich, ox testicles. Outside were wart hogs running around and several giraffes who showed Sue how long their bluish tongues were.

The next day we boarded a small single-engine prop plane to reach the camp in the Maasai Mara Reserve of Kenya. Sue loved the idea that the pilot had to buzz the small landing strip one time to scare the baboons off the runway for us to land safely. We settled into our spacious tent with twin beds and nightstands, a dressing area and three separate partitions with a shower, sink, and commode, all with hot water heated by firewood. I had been in hotel rooms that were less comfortable.

As soon as we were settled, we were off on our first safari with one other couple and our guide/driver. He was great, very knowledgeable and enabled us to see so much more than I expected.

Our Expert Kenya Guide

Not far outside the camp, we encountered a pride of lions who had just killed a zebra. They were busy eating, so they seemed to have no interest in us even though we were only twenty feet away. The females kill the prey; then the male eats first, followed by the females and then the cubs. What a fascinating spectacle.

We returned to our luxurious tent to get ready for dinner. We had to tie the zipper to the tent closed as we left to prevent the monkeys from entering. A tall electrified barbed-wire fence enclosed the camp to protect us from the lions, but the monkeys easily climbed the surrounding trees to drop in.

We first went to the outdoor bar where we could order top-shelf liquor, then to a gourmet outdoor meal. Afterward three men from the Maasai tribes entertained us by dancing and jumping to music. These guys were at least 6 ½ feet tall and they could really jump. We returned to our tent to find hot-water bottles in our beds, which Sue loved. Even though we were at the equator, the daytime temperature was in the 70s and it got chilly at night. That night we heard the roar of the lions and the loud screech of eastern hyraxes (large rodent-looking creatures related to the elephant).

Each day we went on two safari drives, which were amazing. We passed almost two dozen giraffes walking single file nearly 100 yards apart. When we came back, they were in a large circle, facing outward, apparently looking out for their carnivorous enemies. We illegally crossed into the Tanzania Serengeti to see two male lions who had brought down a water buffalo. One was still eating, while the other lay asleep on his back, paws up like a kitten.

We saw the vicious hyenas chase a herd of stupid wildebeest until they caught one and ate it. The many types of antelope were highlighted by the graceful impalas leaping so high one would think there was no gravity. We ventured out on one drive where the guide stopped 25 feet from a small herd of elephants eating grass on both sides of the dirt road. Suddenly, one of the big bull elephants decided he did not like us there. He raised his head, fanned out his ears, let out a load trumpet, and started marching toward us. Our guide immediately backed up, turned around, and quickly drove away, explaining that elephants forewarned a charge exactly as the bull did. We stopped on the way back to see a cheetah resting, perhaps after one of their well-known 75 mile-per-hour chases.

We drove to the bank of the Mara River where 1.3 million wildebeest cross every spring to get to the grasslands. Several of their carcasses were lying along the banks or in the river where they had drowned. Wildebeests are quite stupid and easy prey. Buzzards were plentiful, waiting for a carnivore to rip open wildebeest bodies because the buzzards are unable to do so. In the water were the extremely dangerous hippos and crocodiles. We also saw some water buffalo but did not see the rare black rhino. They are endangered due to poaching.

We arouse early at Sue's insistence to take a hot air balloon ride over the Kenya plain. I was apprehensive about the height until I got into the basket and found the side wall was as high as my armpit. The ride was unexpectedly peaceful as we floated over the Maasai villages and the animals. When we came down, the guides served us a champagne breakfast at our landing spot. It was a welcomed treat.

We visited a tribe's small village, enclosed by rough bramble bushes to keep the lions out. Approximately 30 women stood in a semi-circle and sang to entertain us. Many had their earlobes pierced and stretched, some adorned with beaded ornaments. Afterward we gave them gifts, mostly red garments because the Maasai were known to love red. Then Sue bought their carvings and woven items for mementos. They were happy to get our money. Finally, we were invited into the chief's three-room mud hut. He slept in one room, his wife and children in another, and the tribe's cow in a third. Their standard meal comes from a mixture of cow's milk and blood drained from an opening in the cow's ankle. Their stained teeth revealed their diet. On another day we witnessed an election where the members of many tribes lined up to be counted behind the official that they wish to elect.

We were sorry to leave this interesting adventure into the Maasai Mara. We then flew the short flight back to Nairobi, where we boarded the chartered 737 for the 1,000-mile flight to the Seychelles.

Egypt

After the seven-day cruise around the beautiful Seychelle Islands with their magnificent palm trees and giant granite rocks, we again boarded the charter flight to Egypt. Three weeks earlier, a terrorist band had murdered two busloads of tourists, mostly Germans and Swiss, with the objective of destroying Egyptian tourism. As a result, 45 of our passengers elected to forgo Egypt, proceeding directly back to the United States because they were terrified. So, after the 737 dropped us off at Luxor, it flew them back. Normally Luxor is teaming with tourists, but we 69 were alone and had Luxor to ourselves. We had two guides assigned to our group, both Egyptologists, who impressed us with their knowledge.

Our accommodations were bungalows, which had armed guards patrolling all night to protect us. We rode our bus to the bazaar, and, after shopping late, the bus returned only Sue and me back to our hotel compound. A jeep with four armed guards followed our bus. We felt completely safe.

Drink with Egyptian After Shopping

We spent the morning at the acclaimed outdoor Karnak Temple. The building of the complex began around 2000 BCE and continued until 30 BCE. Only the Giza Pyramids are visited by more tourists in Egypt. Normally over 10,000 people would be here daily. But, because of the terrorist attack, the only people here other than us were a few school children. It is estimated that thirty pharaohs had a hand in Temple design and construction. Inside the walls, the Hypostyle Hall occupies 50,000 square feet with 134 massive columns, including twelve that are 65 feet tall with a diameter of almost ten feet. Across the top are architraves, each weighing 70 tons. Several theories exist as to how these slabs were placed on top, including that the complex was filled with sand, the slabs dragged up to their positions, then the sand excavated. One temple has a 95-foot-high obelisk weighing over 700 tons. Hieroglyphs are present throughout, carved on the pillars, the friezes, and the monuments. Several Hollywood movies featured Karnak as a backdrop.

It was disheartening to visit the Nile River in Luxor. Normally over 100 double-decker river boats would motor up and down the Nile between Luxor and Aswan. Thanks to the terrorist massacre, all these boats were docked four across and their crews laid off. We took a felucca up the river a short distance, enjoyed tea and cake, then sailed back to Luxor, just to get a feel for these old wooden sailboats and to generate some revenue for the owners.

We toured the Valley of the Kings on the west bank of the Nile, then the Valley of the Queens opposite the ancient city of Thebes. We were permitted to view Nefertari's Tomb. She was the favorite wife of Ramses the Second. Her tomb is also called the Sistine Chapel of Ancient Egypt. Usually, it is almost impossible to see because they only allowed 125 people per day, but since we were the only tourists — no problem. Although the tomb, like all the other known tombs, had been looted, the wall paintings were amazing to Sue, including depicting the exquisite features of the ancient queen. The ceiling of the antechamber represented the heavens. The paintings had just been restored and it looked like the artist had just taken a break from his work. The restoration by the Egyptian Antiquities Organization was financed by the Getty Foundation and completed in 1992.

We ventured to the open Hatshepsut Temple, where the terrorist massacres had occurred just three weeks earlier. There were armed guards stationed in sniper positions all around the elevated perimeter. Inside were young Egyptians with a logo on their tee shirts that designated "Down with Terrorism." They gave one to Sue, which she proudly wore. CNN covered their demonstration. Since we were the only tourists present, they interviewed us live on CNN.

Sue persuaded us to take an early-morning flight to Cairo to see the pyramids and the Great Sphinx, another UNESCO World Heritage Site. They are in Giza at the edge of the western desert just outside the sprawling city of Cairo. The Great Pyramid, constructed 2580-2560 BCE, is the oldest of the Ancient Wonders of the World and the only one still in existence.

Not So Ancient Pair Among the Ancient Egyptian Pyramids

Smaller pyramids are nearby. The Great Pyramid is 481 feet tall. Several theories attempted to explain how these tombs for ancient pharaohs were built. Most are based on transporting these giant stones from a quarry on river barges, then dragged up over a sand ramp to be placed precisely. But the grade of the ramp, if linear, would place its foot out into the river. Another is that the ramp wound through the center of the pyramid. We had to fight off vendors at the base of the pyramids trying to get Sue to take a camel ride and to buy their souvenirs. We would have had to pay a ransom to get her back.

The Great Sphinx is 240 feet long and 66 feet high, built around 2500 BCE for the pharaoh Khafre. It was carved into the bedrock of a plateau on the west bank of the Nile within easy walking distance of the Great Pyramid. It is widely considered the world's most wonderful statue. One of our Egyptologist guides published a book that theorized that originally there must have been two Sphinxes, but one was destroyed and eroded away.

The final night in Luxor, the guides put on an authentic Egyptian performance including the Whirling Dervishes. Before we returned to Luxor, we had a cartouche made with Sue's name spelled out in ancient Egyptian symbols. Then we boarded the charter 737 home on a trip we will never forget.

Highlights of Cruising

Although our cruises were not as memorable as the land tours, they offered a great deal of pleasure, if not as much adventure. Obviously, we enjoyed cruising, or we would not have tried it 44 times. Sue loved the food and

This Is Habit-Forming

the casual attire, but she also had fun dressing up for their formal nights. The biggest advantage is seeing wonderful destinations, if only for relatively short times, by not having to pack and unpack throughout the cruise and being pampered.

Initially, our favorite set of cruise ships was the Renaissance line. It began with eight small ships: four with 100 passengers, four with 114. They were more casual with open seating for all meals and no midnight buffets, which suited us. The cabins were ample, and all were suites with balconies. The food was excellent. It was easy to meet people and easier to navigate the shorter hallways. All of this made them perfect for Sue. Best for me, the prices were not too high for what they offered, although somewhat higher than land tours. Eventually Renaissance sold off their small ships, some to private parties, replacing them with eight identical midsize vessels with a capacity of 684 passengers. They were beautifully designed, and we loved them almost as much as the small ships. But Renaissance declared bankruptcy and went out of business on September 25, 2001. Azamara bought three of their ships, Oceania bought four, and Princess bought one.

Our next set of favorite cruises was the Celebrity line. We sailed on several classes of their ships often enough that we received perks, such as access to private rooms for breakfast and cocktail parties. Since they were owned by Royal Caribbean, we also received perks the few times we sailed with them. But Sue did not like ships with over 800 passengers as well. Our ultimate favorite was the Regent Seven Seas line, with which we also received minor perks as frequent guests. We sailed on the lines of other ships, including Windstar, Oceania, Princess, and Crystal. But, except for the Windstar, they never made it into our list of favorites, even though we enjoyed them. With some of these cruises we were joined by friends, as many as three other couples. We also made new friends, six of whom we have since visited in other parts of the country.

Some of the most memorable cruises usually involved some great destinations. A Baltic cruise included three days in Sue's favorite, St. Petersburg, the cultural and historic heart of Russia. Mike, Merle, Don, and Vanda from our country club got together with us to hire a private guide and a driver. This turned out to be a great choice. The guide got us into the Hermitage

Mike, Merle, Vanda, Don, Sue, Kurth

Museum when the crowds were smaller, so we could see almost everything in less than a day. Housed in six buildings, it is the second largest museum in the world next to the Louvre and has the largest collection of art in the world. Our guide also got us into the wine cellar where Rasputin, the mystic and favored friend of the Russian Emperor Nicholas II, was assassinated.

We toured the czar's winter palace and the massive open city square in front. This is where Czar Alexander II was shot in 1879, and the Bolshevik Revolution started in 1917. We toured the palaces of Alexander I and Catherine the Great. Our final visit was St. Basil's Cathedral, within walking distance of our ship. It did not look striking from the outside, but its interior was amazing with malachite green pillars and impressive artwork, a favorite of Sue.

Our first cruise to French Polynesia was on the Windsong, a four-mast sailing ship with only 74 cabins. We could not ask for a more enjoyable cruise. We visited what for Sue were the two most beautiful islands in the world: Bora Bora and Moorea. I agreed. The ship had fun beach toys such as jet skis and snorkeling for the guests. We "swam with the sharks" with the guide feeding them fish just a few feet from our bodies. We also had manta rays brush our ankles while we waded off one of the islands. After the eight-day cruise, we climbed a hill next to the dock to reach a nice restaurant overlooking the Papeete harbor. It was so sad to see our beautiful ship sail away without us and with new passengers. We liked it so much that we took two more cruises to French Polynesia during the next 20 years.

One of my favorite cruise ports in the world is Rio de Janeiro. The first time there we arrived for Carnival, an amazing celebration throughout Rio. Young adults were sleeping in the parks after a long night of celebration; two million people were in the streets. During the day, music appeared throughout the city. We bought Carnival tickets for the first night of the two-day parade by samba schools traversing down the Sambadrome, called the biggest show on earth. Fourteen samba schools prepare for a year with original costumes, music, dance, and floats to compete for $1,000,000 for the winner. Each school begins with fireworks, their music blasting through loudspeakers as 2,000 costume-clad choreographed dancers began their 81-minute, half-mile trek in front of 90,000 spectators for "The Greatest Party on the Planet." Not all were completely clad since the top tiers on their ten gigantic floats displayed topless dancers. Sue deemed it all spectacular. Since it started at 9 PM, we only stayed until 2 AM to see three of the schools perform. I understood why so many young people were sleeping on the grass during the day.

But Rio has more to offer than Carnival. The Ipanema and Copacabana Beaches are world renown. The city views from Sugar Loaf Mountain and Christ the Redeemer are spectacular with houses in valleys running between the many city hills. Sue was in awe. Rio is also famous for hang gliding off the cliffs and for some of the world-famous jewelry stores, where one can stay safe among the petty thieves by being assigned a driver from these stores. Sue

We ascended Sugarloaf Mountain every time we visited Rio.

took advantage of the jewelry wares but not the hang-gliding. We went back to Rio twice more to take in their adventures.

Istanbul, Türkiye became one of our favorite cruise ports. The merchants in 4,000 shops in the Grand Bazaar were entertaining, selling their distinctive carpets, leather clothes, and jewelry. Sue let it be known that she was interested in a black wall hanging. The word spread throughout the bazaar, causing each merchant to show Sue their offerings. We toured the Blue Mosque, the Topkapi Palace, and the Great Mosque. We crossed the Bosporus, the strait that bisects Türkiye and separates Europe from Asia. We took a ferry to the quaint Princes' Islands, where only horse and buggy transportation is allowed.

We were a bit adventurous on our cruise around Cape Horn. We and Merle and Mike started in Santiago Chile, but quickly cruised south for Tierra del Fuego and the northern boundary of the Drake passage where the Pacific and Atlantic meet. This passage is usually rough sailing as the waters around Cape Horn are particularly hazardous and known as one of the major challenges in yachting. But we were fortunate to be able to get through the narrow Strait of Magellan. The cruise ship Celebrity Infinity presented us with certificates to commemorate sailing around Cape Horn and through the Strait. At one of our stops, Sue took a two-hour bus ride to walk among two million penguins. Once again, she demonstrated how much she loved her penguins. We were scheduled to cruise to the Falklands, but the Captain decided the seas were too rough.

Taking a Regent cruise ship through the mighty Amazon River in Brazil and Columbia was unforgettable and a favorite of Sue. Although the Nile is slightly longer (longest in the world), the volume of water through the Amazon is greater than the Mississippi, the Yangtze, and the Nile combined. In the rainy season it discharges 12 million cubic feet-per-second into the Atlantic Ocean. Although several rivers from the mountains on the Western side of South America feed the Amazon, ultimately two major rivers, Rio Negro and Solimoes meet at the largest city on the Amazon: Manaus. These two rivers of different color and density join, but do not mix, displaying a dramatic view of the separate rivers. We both were amazed.

The Amazon rainforest spans over nine countries and is home to 30% of the world's animals and 40,000 plant species. It produces 20% of the world's oxygen. The average annual precipitation is nine feet, spiking to 35 feet in some areas. It is home to the most vivid pink dolphins and the vicious carnivorous piranha, which angler Sue caught with red meat on her hook. The black caiman looks like a large crocodile, but the green anaconda is equally frightening, over 15 feet long. Less visually fearsome, but deadly, are the poison dart frogs which we met in Costa Rica.

Other great cruise stops for us included Dubai, Mumbai, Cape Town, Ho Chi Minh City, Taipei, Buenos Aires, Angkor Wat, Easter Island, the Greek islands, Manila, Crete, Malta, Sicily, the Faroe Islands, Corsica, Cyprus, Gibraltar, Iceland, Dubrovnik, and Alaska. Sue's favorite was Easter Island in the middle of nowhere. The discovery of almost 1,000 Moai statues astonished us. It is still a mystery how such large, heavy statues were excavated and transported to the shore.

Our cruises through the Panama Canal and the St. Lawrence Seaway were also interesting. They first tried to carve the canal through the entire isthmus between the Pacific and Atlantic but abandoned the project after losing many lives. The solution today uses a man-filled lake to traverse most of the journey. This resulted in a much smaller distance for dredging the canal. Our ship went through the locks with only inches of clearance on the sides. Now they have created a canal and locks wide enough for the widest ships to traverse. The St. Lawrence in Canada enabled us to view the many small, white Beluga whales that fascinated Sue.

I left copies of my book, *My 36 Years in Space*, in the libraries of the last Regent and Celebrity ships we sailed. Some readers, including a Regent captain, bought their own copies after reading the ship's copy. I wish I had donated copies to all the ship libraries.

We enjoyed many cruises to the Caribbean islands. They offered the best snorkeling, particularly in the Cayman Islands, Belize, Cozumel, Antigua, and the Virgin Islands. Our favorite was Buck Island adjacent to St. Croix, which John Kennedy named a national monument after he snorkeled there. But Sue insisted the many islands here do not compare to the beauty of French Polynesia or the Hawaiian Islands.

Domestic Travel

I do not want to minimize the great experiences we enjoyed traveling with our friends and family throughout North America. We visited friends in Idaho. We loved the golf course at the Coeur D' Alene Resort where Sue and I were each awarded a certificate for paring their famous island green. The caddy actually had to ferry us to the green in a boat. Now that is a true island green!

We also had a great time with our friends, Bob and Ann Taylor, playing in their couples' member-guest tournament on three wonderful courses in Austin, Texas, including the Ben Crenshaw-designed Barton Creek.

We rented a car with Mike and Merle in Spokane Washington to drive to the beautiful sites in Washington, Montana, and Alberta Canada. We also played at the Banff Springs Golf Course where we stopped to watch a pair of gigantic elk observing us from right off the third green. We spent the night at the Lake Louise Fairmont Hotel, one of Sue's favorites, to take in the surrounding beauty. We drove through a rainy Glacier National Park in Montana for our final destination through the Northwest.

Mike and Merle also accompanied us on a two-week drive through the many wonderful national parks in Utah and Arizona. We first stopped in Sedona to take in the splendor of Sue's colorful bluffs once again. Next, we drove to the Monument Valley Navajo Tribal Park, where Sue sketched the ninety-year-old matriarch in her tent. She created several etchings from these drawings.

Sue's Etching of Navajo Weaver

The hoodoos in Bryce Canyon National Park were the highlight. I stayed on top while the adventurous ones navigated a path though the formations. But the sheer cliffs of Zion were a close second. We also enjoyed Arches National Park, Canyonlands, Capital Reef, the Bridges National Monument, and the Grand Staircase National Monument. There was something for everyone.

Sue and Merle at Zion

The Grand Canyon, Our Favorite

Of course, our favorite of the West was always the Grand Canyon. Sue and I consumed its splendor every chance we had. The last time we hired a helicopter to take us from Las Vegas to the bottom of the canyon was amazing. While the ride was thrilling, the natural beauty and majesty of the canyon was incomparable.

We celebrated our special wedding anniversaries with our family. For our 45th, we bought a package at the Los Caballeros dude ranch in Wickenburg, Arizona for the ten of us, playing golf, riding horses, getting massages, playing tennis, and swimming. An astronomer gave us a telescope show, and we went on a hayride, listening to a guitar-playing singer for the nighttime entertainment.

Flowered leis highlighted our 50th anniversary.

For our 50th anniversary we rented three villas for our three families in Wailea, Maui. They bought us flowered leis, which we displayed all week.

We rented surfboards, golf clubs, snorkeling equipment, and bicycles to ride down from the Haleakala Crater. In the evening, our families invited us to their villas for dinner. On the night of our 50th anniversary, they sent us off to a local luau. We will never forget that special week.

Special Cake from the Kids on Our Special Day

Pam, Karissa, Rachel, Scott, Griffin, Kurth, Sue, Sean, Sheryl, Taylor

Sue and I also had great Hawaiian golfing vacations on our own in Oahu, Kauai, Maui, and the Big Island. Especially memorable were the beauty of Hanalei Bay, the rough road to Hana, the helicopter ride over the Kilauea lava flow, the six memorable golf courses in Wailea, Kapalua, and Makena, and the snorkeling in the semi-submerged Molokini crater. Mauni Lani and Mauni Kea were breath-taking.

We took an escorted 24-person Tauck tour through the Bourbon Trail. It began at Churchill Downs in Kentucky. Sue loved listening to anecdotes from a retired jockey as we watched the horses on the track. We visited the Kentucky bourbon distilleries along the Bourbon Trail on our way through the Smokey Mountains. We spent the night in the famous Biltmore Hotel in Asheville, North Carolina. We ended up enjoying the Grand Ole Opry near Nashville and were treated to a private serenade by a Nashville song writer.

We visited our son's family in Alexandria Virginia several times. We never tire of touring our nation's capital: the National Mall, the Smithsonian Air and Space Museum, the Lincoln Memorial, the war memorials, the Washington Monument, and the Air Force Memorial. No American should miss these great sites.

Of course, we found New York City a great place to visit. We saw the World Trade Center Twin Towers before their destruction and visited the 9/11 Memorial afterward. Little Italy, Chinatown, Central Park, Rockefeller Center, Radio City Music Hall, and Times Square are all worth a visit. For Sue, the best are the Broadway musicals. Somehow, they seem more exciting in New York than Southern California.

Our cruises through Alaska were also unforgettable. We loved observing the caving in Glacier Bay, taking a helicopter ride to the Mendenhall Glacier, walking on it, and

Helicopter to Mendenhall Glacier

watching Sue zipline at Icy Strait Point. Enjoying a beer at a bar in little towns of Juneau, Skagway, and Ketchikan was fun. Denali is spectacular.

We also enjoyed a driving trip with Mike and Merle through New Mexico. We did miss some important sites, but the Indian culture inspired some of Sue's etchings. High winds prevented the launching of the hot air balloons in Albuquerque. We were not permitted to visit the famous Taos Pueblo due to a tribal funeral. We bypassed the wonderful Carlsbad Caverns because we had taken our children there in 1975. Still, we had a good trip, learning about and seeing the exhibits at the Indian Pueblo Culture Center, taking the tramway to Sandia Peak in Albuquerque, and dining at Vernon's Speakeasy. Sue found this place surreptitiously, obtaining the password from a departing guest. A bouncer opened the viewing slot in a large black wooden door under a red light to receive our password, then welcomed us while holding a baseball bat. The place was dark, prices unexpectedly high, and the epitome of a prohibition speakeasy of the past. I inferred from the magazines in the lobby that this speakeasy may be peddling marijuana.

On our last domestic flight, we had a horrible experience on American Airlines. First, we waited over six hours to learn our flight was cancelled because they were one slight attendant short. American could not book a flight home from New Orleans for two days. They had no vouchers left for hotel accommodations or food. We were on our own. We finally booked two nights at a downtown casino. Two days later, we boarded our first class seats to Orange County, connecting in Dallas. But after boarding in Dallas, the head flight attendant forced Sue to check her carry-on. We could not understand why until we returned home to discover her pouch of expensive jewelry was missing from the carry-on. We never recovered the $40,000 value. We never booked American Airlines again.

11.   The Granny

It looked as if Sheryl would be unable to conceive, The doctors believed the problem was the absence of eggs. So, when Sean decided to leave his accounting role as a CPA with Deloitte & Touche to start a new company, Sheryl was teaching elementary school in Huntington Beach. Since starting a family was not imminent, they could live on Sheryl's salary while Sean could forgo compensation from the new startup. Then a miracle happened. Sheryl became pregnant! Sean's mother, Liisa, produced a plan: the grandmothers could take care of the baby during the weekday hours that Sheryl was teaching. Sue loved the plan. She took care of the baby 1-2 days each week with Liisa responsible for the other days. Sue could curtail her OT hours, philanthropy activities and artist responsibilities to do something she loved even more.

Taylor was born on April 23, 1994, a beautiful, happy, cuddly, miracle baby. We were all elated. The plan worked well. Sue and Liisa enjoyed taking care of Taylor. Sheryl and Sean relished the weekends when they embraced her full time. Baby Taylor seemed to enjoy all the attention. Sean's business got off to a good start.

Taylor grew into a gregarious, personable toddler, dancing and showing off for her grandmothers at every opportunity. It was clear that she loved her Granny and her Grandma. A highlight was every birthday and Christmas. Sue would take Taylor shopping. They spent hours together choosing just the right gifts, wrapping them, and having lunch. These

Fun-loving Taylor at Age 4

became a tradition that lasted even as Taylor became an adult. Sue was especially proud to attend her graduation from Baylor since her choice of major graphic design coincided with Sue's profession.

Kurth, Liisa, Sheryl, Scott, Rachel, Taylor, Karissa, Sue, Bob, Pam

Taylor was four-years old when Sheryl again tried to conceive without success. She even flew to the East Coast to see a specialist only to learn another baby would not be possible. So, they looked into several adoption options. A single mother with two daughters was pregnant and looking for qualified parents to adopt her forthcoming baby. She did not know who the father was. But Sean and Sheryl had competition for the adoption. We were told that another well-qualified couple was vying for adopting the baby. We all met at Sheryl's home to meet the prospective mother. We knew of the competition and considered the opportunity as an interview. We convinced the mother that her baby would be best with all of us. Sue played an important part in this interview.

So, Griffin was born on June 28, 1999. Sheryl was in the delivery room to receive him. Taylor was so excited to now have a baby brother to play with. But he apparently wasn't ready for playtime with a sophisticated five-year-old. Disenchanted, Taylor told Sue, "All he does is eat, sleep, and poop."

Griffin revealed his intelligence to Granny at an early age. He was two-years-old when Sue saw him assembling Transformer figures. He could not read as yet, so he created the assemblies from the pictures. When he was three, he showed Granny how to transform the parts from a vehicle to an action figure.

One morning, Sue was up early and went into the garage for something, but locked herself in. She called four-year-old Griffith to wake up Grandpa to free her. But Griffin said, "I can fix it." He retrieved

Griffin the Contractor

a screwdriver and hammer and began to remove the garage door.

Griffin the Toolman

Granny didn't have to read to Griffin once he learned how. He was a voracious reader and read as many as 40 books in a summer.

Four-Year-Old Griffin

But Scott and Pam started their family for Granny a full year before Sheryl and Sean did. Sue was absolutely thrilled when Rachel was born to Scott and Pam in

Chandler Arizona on April 22, 1993. We couldn't wait to meet our first grandchild.

Baby Rachel arrives, We are now Grandpatents!

Sue decided to have all the grandchildren call her Granny, which they do even today, although they are all adults.

Rachel at Five Years

Karissa was born August 15, 1994, in Tucson Arizona. They lived remotely, moving for Scott's deployments, so Sue's exposure to them was not frequent, Nevertheless they developed a strong attachment to Granny.

Karissa at Two Years

Four Wonderful Grandchildren: Griffin, Karissa, Rachel, Taylor,

We attended Rachel's graduation from James Madison University and Karissa's from Regent College. We were so proud. Rachel graduated Suma Cum Laude. Karissa was the school's unofficial social chairman.

Taylor, Rachel, Kurth, Sue, Griffin, Karissa

Granny acquired the love and respect of each of our four grandchildren.

12. The Surgery Patient

Sue successfully endured 17 major surgeries in her adult life. Two were to remove overactive parathyroid glands that were destroying her kidneys. Three surgeries were required to remove gallstones, then to remove the gall bladder, then to repair the stint. Two more were to repair deformities in her feet. One was to repair her bladder; In 2016 she was diagnosed with breast cancer. She underwent a lumpectomy in addition to radiation treatments and chemotherapy. But she had to cease the chemo because it was affecting her already damaged kidneys.

Four years later, Sue's nephrologist informed her that her kidneys were dying, and she needed to undergo dialysis soon. He told her not to try getting on the waiting list for a kidney transplant because she was too old (age 69). Neither our children nor I had the same blood type, so we were excluded. A friend from church, Dennis O'Hare, had the same blood type and volunteered one of his kidneys. The head nephrologist at UCLA asserted he was too old to donate at age 69. Dennis insisted he was in excellent health as a runner and mountain climber, convincing the doctors he would be a good candidate. The nephrologist acquiesced and began a series of tests. Dennis passed the first set of tests and was proclaimed an excellent donor candidate. But a later test disqualified him because he had too many arteries and veins emanating from his kidneys.

We were devastated. Sue's father had lived eight years on dialysis, which was unusually long. But a nurse at UCLA informed us of a website, "Matching Donors.com," which tries to match live kidney donors (and liver donors) with needy patients. We jumped at it and donated the $600 to post Sue's need. We submitted a narrative as to why she deserved a kidney and posted the prettiest picture of Sue. The website states boldly in large letters that there is a $50,000 fine or five years in jail for buying or selling a kidney. We were surprised and overjoyed to acquire six hits. UCLA convinced us not to respond to the two: from England and from South Africa, because we would pay to fly them here, but would never see them again. We did reach out to a 25-year-old man from Ada Oklahoma and a middle aged woman from California.

Robert Chiles responded that he was willing to donate one of his kidneys in remembrance of his grandmother who passed aways due to kidney failure. He submitted a blood test to prove a match with Sue's. We were permitted to legally pay all his expenses and to compensate him for any loss of income during his absence. We flew him to Las Angeles to undergo the necessary testing at UCLA. He was declared a 98% match!

While he was en route, someone alerted us to a website that gave us a clue as to what might have been a primary motive for his willingness to donate a kidney. The website said that Robert was in trouble with the law. He founded a LBGTQ organization in Oklahoma, then embezzled $10,000 from it. He was not yet in court, but his trial was pending. We surmised the kidney donation may have been a gesture to demonstrate his good character. While he stayed in our home for three days, we were careful not to leave him alone.

This was his first time in California, so we really showed him around. We took him to the Pacific Ocean, to the Long Beach aquarium, to the Nixon Presidential Library, to the Griffith Park planetarium, to the UCLA campus, to Hollywood, and to our daughter's home to meet her family. What he most enjoyed in Griffith Park was his ability to see the Hollywood sign. And he was very excited about the Hollywood Walk of Fame, where he took at least 200 pictures of the entertainment stars featured on the pavement.

He promised to return for the scheduled kidney transplant. He took two large jugs of seawater and a Bird of Paradise plant home to show his relatives. During his stay we learned that he had told us several fibs about his employment to embellish the compensation we reimbursed for missing work. We were also concerned that he may get cold feet and not return. Meanwhile we prepared Sue for minor surgery for peritoneal dialysis requiring a tube to be inserted in her stomach. Her kidneys were clearly failing. But the doctors wanted to hold off in case she could wait it out for the imminent transplant.

But Robert did return for the surgery as scheduled. He brought his 17-year-old cousin for support. The head nephrologist at UCLA met with us for a final consultation the day before. He ordered the cousin and me out of the room so that he could grill Robert. He asked Robert why he was doing this? How much money did I offer him? How was I coercing him? Robert started to cry before he finally let Robert go.

But we had one more hurdle to overcome; the hospital told us Sue would require many expensive medications for the rest of her life, and they needed assurance that we could afford the meds, including the anti-injection medication.

That afternoon, I told Robert that I would happily take him wherever he wanted in southern California. He and his cousin wanted to return to the Hollywood Walk of Fame. I parked there and told them I would wait in the car, but they could take as long as they desired.

After two hours they returned excited. They witnessed John Stamos getting his star. So, they took many pictures of the ceremony in addition to more pictures of the permanent stars embedded in the pavement. Then they wanted to see Rodeo Drive in Beverly Hills. Again, I stayed in the car as they went through the shops, taking pictures of themselves trying on expensive purses and having a gay-old time.

Scott and Sheryl accompanied us for the operation the next day. Scott stayed by Robert's bed to comfort him both before and after the surgery. Sheryl and I stayed with Sue. The surgical team was ready to administer dialysis in case it was necessary. Sue's kidneys were functioning at 5% at the time. The operation was 100% successful! I could immediately see how well the new kidney inserted in her abdomen was working. I wanted to cheer. Sue's new kidney turned out to be the healthiest organ in her body. It actually got stronger over the years.

Sue was discharged a day before Robert was. They both recuperated well in our home. We put Robert and his cousin on the plane several days later. We told him that he was now an additional member of the family. Indeed, Sue sent him presents on holidays in perpetuity.

Sue and Robert Recovering from Their Kidney Transplant Surgery

But he did finally admit to his troubles with the law. The letters we sent to the judge and the lawyers proclaiming his altruism, basically seeking leniency, were ignored. He received a seven year sentence for a white collar crime. He served 3½ years before being released on parole. I could hardly believe the harshness until I read John Grisham's only non-fiction book, "The Innocent Man." It revealed the callousness and severity of the criminal justice system in Ada, Oklahoma.

Sue underwent a hip replacement in 2017. As usual, she was an excellent patient and did all the exercises suggested by the surgeon to strengthen the surrounding muscles prior to the procedure. She recovered quickly. The doctor was pleased and told her she was under no restrictions. She could do anything she desired. Unfortunately, she believed him. A few days later she wanted to replace the Thanksgiving pumpkins on our balcony with Christmas decorations, So, she through her leg over the balcony railing and dislocated her new hip. The ambulance took her to emergency, where after two tries they finally relocated her new hip. At this point, the doctor DID give her restrictions, causing her to give up golf after 70 years.

Epilogue

Sue's routine blood test showed a positive cancer marker. She immediately assumed her breast cancer 21 years ago had returned. But several tests later showed they were clear. Our initial relief was short-lived as we realized the cancer was elsewhere. A PET scan indicated significant liver cancer. The doctors believed it must have metastasized from another body source, but after upper and lower GIs, they concluded it was isolated to the liver. We scheduled surgery for October 26, 2023, at Hoag Hospital.

As we walked into the hospital, I told her that I wished it were me instead of her. She knew I was serious and thanked me, telling me how strong I was. The hepatologist told us the cancer had spread to half the liver which would have to be removed, but because the liver is able to regenerate, one can live with as little as 20% of a healthy liver. He told us to expect one day in intensive care, followed by one week in the hospital, followed by 1-2 weeks in rehabilitation as an outpatient.

Sheryl accompanied me to Sue's bedside, so we were there when she woke up. Although she seemed okay even under the anesthesia, Sue announced to us that she was dead! After much convincing, she seemed surprised, and announced she was alive! The next day, the physical therapist put her in a bed lounge chair and wheeled her into another room for a better view of the ocean outside. But she was not ready to leave the ICU. The surgeon came by to tell us he had to take out more of her liver than expected. He appeared very grave with this announcement. Later, they opened her up again to insert a stint to allow the liver to drain better. Sheryl and I kept assuring her that she was improving. But she remained in the ICU. The physical therapist no longer paid a visit. Scott flew from Virginia and joined Sheryl and me at her bedside for eleven days, but then he had to return home for business. Although Sue was no longer opening her eyes without prompting, she heard every word we said. She smiled when I told her how much I loved her.

During her stay in the hospital, I received an overwhelming number of get-well cards from our friends and neighbors. I received flowers, lilies and amaryllis from some. People invited me to dinner at their homes and brought me food they had baked for me.

I had called our astronaut friends, Charlie and Dotty Duke to let them know of Sue's condition. The next day they called from their vacation in Switzerland. Sue acknowledged their conversation with smiles and nods when I put the phone to her ear.

Sue's favorite music genre was country and western. She especially liked Kenny Rogers. We attended his final concert. So, I softly sang these songs to Sue.

One day, Tayor and Karissa joined Sheryl in the ICU.

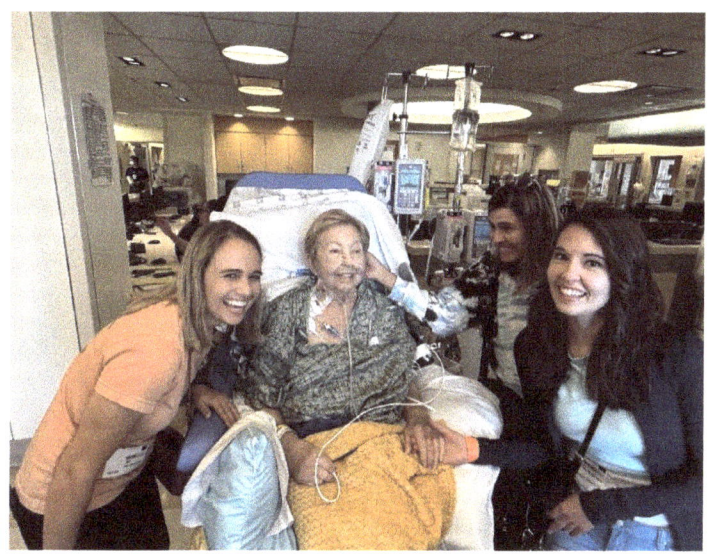

Sue was smiling even to the end.

But she was not improving. At one point she announced that she wanted to die. Over the years we had discussed end-of-life options. We both agreed that quality of life was paramount. We each created a Durable Power of Attorney for Healthcare that stipulated not invoking extraordinary measures for life saving procedures and contained a Do Not Resuscitate command. She did have a tube through her mouth to her stomach transmitting nutrients since she was not permitted to swallow for fear of aspiration. She also had a tube providing oxygen through her nostrils. But apparently this violated her wishes as she pulled both out three times, until she was restrained.

She repeatedly told Sheryl and me that she wanted to die. Hard as this was for both of us, we acquiesced when the hospital staff suggested it was time for Sue to be put in hospice. I asked her to save a place for me in heaven. I promised her a wonderful Celebration of Life service.

Sue passed away peacefully on November 20, 2023, after being in the hospital 25 days. Sheryl and I were at her side every day.

The outpouring of condolences was overwhelming. Reata Glen set her photograph announcing her passing outside the Residence Services Vestibule for nine days. Later, they permitted posting her picture announcing the Celebration of Life services December 7 at South Shores Church.

Susan Krause

of Reata Glen passed away on November 20, 2023, at the age of 83. Sue was born on February 25, 1940, in Fond du Lac, Wisconsin, where she grew up. She met Kurth on the student train coming out for the University of Wisconsin 1960 Rose Bowl. Their first date was Disneyland.

One year later, Sue became the First Lady of Kurth's fraternity. They were engaged after Sue received her bachelor's degree in occupational therapy. They were married one year later on June 15, 1963. Sue began employment as an OTR when she completed her internship. She employed her skills to treat mentally ill children in a pilot program at Milwaukee County General Hospital.

Two years later she left the profession to begin a family as a stay-at-home mom. Scott was born June 9, 1965, in Milwaukee. They moved to Boston, Massachusetts when Kurth accepted a position to work on the Apollo program at MIT. Their second child, Sheryl, was born in Lynn, Massachusetts, March 31, 1967.

In September they moved to Houston, where Kurth supported the Apollo program for the next eight years. Sue made lifelong friends with wives of the Apollo astronauts. Using her art minor, she became a professional artist, specializing in limited edition, hand-pulled etchings. Ultimately, her work was featured in eleven galleries across the USA. She published a featured article in a national fine arts magazine for graphic artists.

They moved to Costa Mesa, CA, in 1975. Sue served as a deacon at St. Andrew's Presbyterian Church. She led a committee, called Four Score and More, to provide an annual luncheon for the church's 400 octogenarians. In the 1980's, Sue was a member of the Board of Directors for the annual fashion show at Children's Hospital of Orange County, which she chaired. She was a member of the Las Alleger's Woman's Group in Costa Mesa. Sue was president of the professionally juried Art-A-Fair in Laguna Beach as well as the Costa Mesa Art League. In 1997, Sue returned to her profession as an occupational therapist serving nursing homes in California until her retirement in 2001. They moved to their Reata Glen retirement community in 2019.

Sue loved to play golf, which she did for 68 years, and, to travel. When the kids were in college, they obtained their passports and began the many adventures that Sue loved. She and Kurth sailed on 44 cruises and visited 99 countries. Her favorites were Japan, Israel, United Arab Emirates, Egypt, Singapore, Kenya, the Seychelles, Easter Island and the Tahitian Islands.

Sue was a loving, devoted wife of 60 years, a dedicated mother, and a proud grandmother, deeply loved by all. She had countless wonderful friends. We will all miss her caring demeanor, love for life and for Jesus, and her winning smile.

PRELUDE
Music by Beth Williams

WELCOME & OPENING PRAYER
Pastor Ty Guy

"HOW GREAT IS OUR GOD"
Congregational sing along

SHARING BY FAMILY AND FRIENDS

SUSAN'S LIFE IN PICTURE VIDEO
By Taylor Odish

THOUGHTS AND MEDITATIONS
Pastor Ty Guy

"AMAZING GRACE"

CLOSING PRAYER
Pastor Ty Guy

RECEPTION
Please join the family at a reception immediately following the service in the Ocean Room.

Sheryl worked with the church to plan the service and High Tea afterward. The Reata Glen neighbors sent an abundance of flowers to adorn the church sanctuary. Prior to the service, Paster Ty accompanied Scott, Sheryl, Sandy and her nephew, Jeff, on a boat which took us three miles into the Pacific Ocean to scatter her ashes among flower petals. We returned to the church to find many already lining up. The organist played "How Great is Our God" and "Amazing Grace" in addition to Sue's favorite "Unchained Melody." More than 175 people attended, even though the church staff cautioned that 100 would be a good estimate. Even our good friends, Mike and Merle Moshiri, flew out from Florida to attend. Scott, Sheryl, Taylor, and Sue's best friends from Reata Glen, Becky Larsen and Jane Franz, gave beautiful eulogies. Sheryl electrified the crowd wearing and changing into three of Sue's iconic jackets during her presentation. Many told me personally that this was the best Celebration of Life they had ever attended. They all helped fulfill my promise to Sue for a special ceremony. All but a few attended the High Tea reception following the service. Fortunately, the caterer saw how the church was filling up and called for the additional food. I was happy to write the additional checks.

Subsequently, the immediate relatives gathered at our home. I let them know how proud and thankful I was for their participation. I know Sue would be grateful. But knowing Sue, she may have been embarrassed by all the attention.

All the flowers were brought to my porch, filling the entry alcove. I asked exactly the right person what to do with all these flowers. Unknown to me, Becky was a florist. She spent the next three days separating them into bouquets and placing them into vases. I distributed some to our neighbors. I placed the largest arrangement with Sue's picture back at the Residence Services vestibule.

Reata Glen Display of Sue's Celebration of Life Program Among Becky's Flower Arrangement

A few months later after we began recovering from the grief, I invited many of the neighbors and friends to select from the stylish jackets which epitomize Sue's persona. I distributed 74 jackets to those of similar size. Becky decided to honor Sue and her famous jackets with a photograph of the recipients in the Reata Glen concert hall. Multiple photographs were required to capture all of them. Today I see her jackets all around the campus.

One of Three Pictures of Reata Glen Residents Displaying Sue's Jackets

I also invited several residents to Sue's art studio to select one of the dozens of etchings she had pulled but never put up for sale. All were thrilled to frame and hang them in their homes. Becky is planning a house-to-house visit to view the framed etchings on the next anniversary of Sue's birth.

So, I am still recovering and attended a series of Grief Share meetings at South Shores Church. I miss my love, my wife, and my best friend. I am so grateful that God gave me 60 amazing years with this incredible woman. I hope Sue has saved a place for me so we can eventually reunite.

My Special Lady in Her Usual Smile and Accessories.

Bibliography

Charlie & Dotty Duke, *Moonwalker*, Oliver Nelson Books, Nashville, TN, 1990.

Krause, Kurth, *My 36 Years in Space: An Astronautical Engineer's Journey through the Triumphs and Tragedies of America's Space Programs,* third edition, Costa Mesa, CA, 2019.

Krause, Kurth, *Choices: A Roadmap through Life,* Rancho Mission Viejo, CA, 2020.

Strobel, Lee, *The Case for Christ,* Zondervan, Grand Rapids Michigan, 1998.

www.ingramcontent.com/pod-product-compliance
Lightning Source LLC
Chambersburg PA
CBHW051545010526
44118CB00022B/2587